The Once and Future Democrats

PAUL SIMON

THE
ONCE AND
FUTURE
DEMOCRATS

Strategies for Change

CONTINUUM · NEW YORK

To my daughter and son, Sheila and Martin,
whose children and children's children
will be affected by our response or failure to respond

1982
The Continuum Publishing Company
575 Lexington Avenue
New York, N.Y. 10022

Printed in the United States of America

Library of Congress Cataloging in Publication Data

Simon, Paul, 1928–
  The once and future Democrats.

  Includes bibliographical references and index.
  1. Democratic Party (U.S.) 2. United States —
Politics and government — 1981–   I. Title.
JK2317 1982.S53   324.2736   81-19630
ISBN 0-8264-0202-X   AACR2

Contents

Introduction

" "Where do we go from here?" many confused and dismayed Democrats asked after the devastating results of the 1980 election. Part of the postelection discussion concerned substantive matters: What do we stand for as a party and what should we stand for? That goes to the heart and soul of the Democratic party and of the nation. I will explore that question in these pages.

Many policy areas cannot be examined in a quick overview such as this. I will not deal with the highly volatile abortion issue, nor with the almost unknown issue of where we will get zinc — nor many other issues between that *A* and *Z*. The guiding principle in the areas I do examine holds for any policy area: compassion tempered by common sense. And the phrase *common sense* must include much greater stress on quality in performance throughout our culture as well as more emphasis on productivity.

Part of the discussion of the future of the Democratic party inevitably moves to methodology: How does the party use television more effectively? What can be done about corporate political action committees and their mushrooming campaign contributions? How can the tools of direct mail be used as our competitors on the Right have done so effectively? These and other questions of methodology are not the focus of this book. By not examining them, however, I do not intend to downplay their importance.

When someone referred to Indian treaties during a congressional hearing recently, it occurred to me that I had never read one of the treaties between the United States and the various Indian tribes. I asked a staff member to get me some and I read twenty treaties. Not only do these documents show little generosity on the part of the United States government, but even worse, sometimes we have half forgotten and ignored our side of the bargain. In the 1804 treaty with the Delawares, we agreed to employ people "to teach them to make fences." I am sure there were valid reasons for making that a major educational aim in 1804. In 1982, however, Indians have a heritage that includes paternalism, neglect, and indifference on the part of the United States. They don't need people to teach them to make fences, but they want a shared sense of concern and opportunity.

The Democratic party has an unwritten treaty with the American people that is almost as old as that treaty with the Delaware Indians. Yesterday's needs are not necessarily today's, but people do want to feel that the Democratic party is genuinely concerned, that it is not simply serving itself, that it is expanding the opportunities for the young and old of the nation. And when, every two years, the nation determines whether to renew its treaty with the Democrats or with the Republicans, if Democrats do not convey a sense of caring combined with common sense, then Republicans prevail. What the Democratic party needs — what the nation needs — is not an avalanche of additional information. We generally have adequate data to make decisions. The question is one of attitude. The oldest political party in the land must neither automatically embrace nor automatically reject the decisions of the past. But Democrats dare not reject the tradition of concern.

The budget proposals of President Reagan were put together without asking a fundamental question: What will be the impact on the quality of life? That quality-of-life question, which the president addresses only indirectly — and Democrats have not addressed adequately — cannot be brushed aside. That question must be approached thoughtfully in all areas of national life. And the quality of life cannot be improved with mediocrity of performance, whether in the presidency or in the pulpit, in the Congress or in the counting house, in the schoolroom or in the steel mill, on the farm or in the fast-food chain.

There is a danger that an articulate president such as Ronald Reagan, who knows how to lead, can become a Pied Piper for the Democratic party. His tune is mesmerizing, but he is leading in the wrong direction. Woodrow Wilson set out the task in his first inaugural address: "Our duty is to cleanse, to reconsider, to restore, to correct the evil without impairing the good, to purify and humanize every process of our common life without weakening or sentimentalizing it."[1]

Acknowledgments

This book is a call to the Democratic party to correct our deficiencies, but not to sell our soul.

I am grateful to many people for their help on one or more portions of this book. They include Victoria Otten, John Marty, Milton Katz, Judy Wagner, Leo Ribuffo, Representative Thomas Downey, Representative Stephen Solarz, Representative Berkley Bedell, Representative Phillip Sharp, Jack Jennings, Paul Morrill, Jean Peters, Joe Dunn, Leon Keyserling, and Karl Kindel. Thanks also go to my brother, Arthur Simon, critic of all my writings; my daughter Sheila, a junior at Wittenberg University, who seemed to enjoy correcting her father; my wife, Jeanne, who not only read the manuscript but tolerated the life that goes with writing one; Vicki Coupling, who typed the first and succeeding drafts without complaint; Jeannette Hopkins, my editor, who is not only a superb craftsman but a believer in the cause about which I write; and Michael Leach, my publisher at Continuum, who has been encouraging throughout the process. What is in this book is enriched by these people, but the conclusions and responsibility are mine.

CHAPTER ONE

The Meaning of the 1980 Elections

T he 1980 elections had a clear result: a substantial loss for the Democrats at every level of government. Why did it happen?

Sometimes we look for complex answers and miss the obvious. I carried my southern Illinois district by a slim majority of 2,085 votes after winning it by 52,535 in 1978. After the election my wife and I drove back to Washington. When we travel we frequently leave the interstate highways to drive through the countryside and small towns, getting a different perspective of the nation than the effortless drive on massive ribbons of concrete gives us.

In Crofton, Kentucky (population 823), we stopped at a small Exxon service station. I asked the man and his wife who operate the station by themselves how they had voted. "I hate to split my ticket," he replied. "But we had to do something about inflation. I'm a Democrat, but I voted for Reagan. Four years ago I'm afraid we sent a boy to do a man's job." That was it. No ideology. No repudiation of party affiliation. Just an expression of common sense as he saw it by a middle-aged man from Crofton, Kentucky. He sensed correctly that inflation was a major problem and that the administration in power was not tackling it vigorously. He wanted practical answers to problems.

Surveys indicate only slight change in fundamental philosophy in recent years, though they show a drop in identification with the Democratic party. In spite of remarkably little shift on issues over the last decade, in 1972, 47 percent of the electorate identified themselves as Democrats compared with 38 percent in 1980; Republicans, 22 percent in 1972 and 26 percent in 1980; "independents," 26 percent in 1972 and 38 percent in 1980. In 1974, 31 percent called themselves liberal and, in 1980, 26 percent; conservative, 30 percent in 1974 and 34 percent in 1980; moderate, 40 percent in 1974 and 41 percent in 1980.[1] The polls show more change in party identification than in attitude on issues or in how people view their own philosophy. The July 1981 polls by Harris and Gallup indicated slight gains for the Democrats in political-party preferences and some shift away from identification with the word *liberal* and further identification with the label *conservative*, though when the phrase *right of center* is used rather than *conservative,* there is a drop in identification rather than an increase. And when questioned on issues, in any poll there are those who identify themselves as conservative but nonetheless favor making government-sponsored health services available to everyone, to use one of many possible examples.

Despite talk of "an overwhelming election mandate," a study of the election statistics shows results considerably less clear-cut than is commonly perceived. Reagan got slightly less than 51 percent of the vote — not exactly an overwhelming mandate. The Republicans unexpectedly captured the Senate, but if you total the votes for senatorial candidates, the Democrats come out ahead 52 percent to 48 percent. All of the liberal Democratic senators ran appreciably ahead of their more conservative presidential candidate, Jimmy Carter. Senators up for reelection led Carter by these percentages:

Birch Bayh (Indiana)	8%
Dale Bumpers (Arkansas)	11%
Frank Church (Idaho)	24%
Alan Cranston (California)	18%
John Culver (Iowa)	7%
John Durkin (New Hampshire)	20%
Thomas Eagleton (Missouri)	8%
Wendell Ford (Kentucky)	17%
John Glenn (Ohio)	30%
Gary Hart (Colorado)	20%
Ernest Hollings (South Carolina)	24%
Daniel Inouye (Hawaii)	33%
Patrick Leahy (Vermont)	12%
Warren Magnuson (Washington)	8%
George McGovern (South Dakota)	7%
Robert Morgan (North Carolina)	3%
Gaylord Nelson (Wisconsin)	5%

Comparisons between states are somewhat unfair, because some have straight-party circles or levers, while many do not. With the possible exceptions of Robert Morgan and Wendell Ford, all of these senators would be judged to be more liberal than Jimmy Carter, and a strong argument could be made that these two should be ranked more liberal also. Only one incumbent Democratic senator ran behind the president, Senator Herman Talmadge, who lost in Georgia with 49 percent, while the president carried his home state with 56 percent of the vote. There the Senate censure for Talmadge's handling of money (as well as his personal life) clearly dominated, not political philosophy.

A state-by-state analysis of House races shows much the same results; no clear ideological patterns emerge. In the Virginia districts of Democratic Representatives Herbert Harris and Joseph Fisher, roughly one-fourth of those who voted for Reagan voted for the more liberal Democratic congressional candidates.

In Oregon, the most conservative of the Oregon Democratic House members, Representative Al Ullman, lost, but his more liberal colleagues won. In California, one of the most liberal House Democrats, Representative James Corman, lost, but so did two of the most conservative members of the Democratic delegation in that state.

Those who read either sweeping conservative or liberal trends into the election misread it, with one exception: the South. The results do reflect a greater swing to conservatism and a growing Republican strength in the southern states. It is probably no mere coincidence that these states are the heart of the support for the group that calls itself the Moral Majority. The southern states now have a divided 11-11 representation in the Senate, where twenty years ago it was 22-0 in favor of the Democrats.

Virginia, once a bastion of the Democratic party, has a conservative Democratic governor as a result of the 1981 election after a lengthy period of Republican domination of the executive mansion, but in its entire Senate and House delegation has only one Democrat, Representative Dan Daniel, a conservative former commander of the American Legion. In North Carolina, Senator Robert Morgan lost unexpectedly to a much more conservative and little-known opponent. Two highly respected members of the North Carolina House Democratic delegation, Representatives Lamar Gudger and Richardson Preyer, lost to more conservative Republican candidates.

Even within states the southern conservative swing is apparent. Illinois, for example, is considered a northern state, yet the southern part of the state had strong Confederate and proslavery sentiments during the Civil War and pre–Civil War years. That area of Illinois followed the 1980 southern conservative trend. Its southernmost district, which I represent, is geographically much closer to Jackson, Mississippi, than to Chicago; it is south of Louisville, Kentucky, and Richmond, Virginia. Culturally, it is southern also.

In 1976 Jimmy Carter won my congressional district, 127,696 to Gerald Ford's 109,391; Carter carried sixteen of twenty-two counties in rural southern Illinois. In 1980 Ronald Reagan carried twenty-one of those twenty-two counties, winning by a margin of 131,012 to 95,294. But in the northern part of Illinois, the results were much different. In 1976 Jimmy Carter defeated Gerald Ford in Cook County (Chicago) 54 to 46 percent; in 1980 Carter increased that lead slightly to 57 percent against Reagan's 43 percent. In the Cook County city-suburban district of Representative Marty Russo, Jimmy Carter lost in 1976, 58 to 42 percent, but won in 1980, 51 to 49 percent.[2]

How much of the southern conservative tilt is caused by economic factors, how much by the religious right wing; how much is simply a reflection of heavy political spending, how much of an older and more conservative population that has moved south — all these are factors, but how each should be weighed is not clear. There is also an element that some writers call "the new conservatism," voters and groups not concerned with the traditional social issues but rather with such issues as gun control, abortion, school prayer, or busing. These single-issue voters became convinced, to a great extent by what they received through the mail, that there was a substantial difference between the two parties on these issues, often creating issues where there were none.

Outside of the South, there were no clear electoral trends. North and South Dakota and Nevada provide the most dramatic examples of swings with no discernible pattern. In Nevada, Carter dropped from 47 percent of the vote to 27 percent between 1976 and 1980. Yet in that same state, moderate Democratic Congressman Jim Santini, Nevada's lone House member, won with 68 percent of the vote, while Republican Senator Paul Laxalt, a conservative by any standards, received a 58 percent vote. In North Dakota, Carter also dropped 20 percent from 1976; Representative Mark Andrews, not part of the most conservative wing of his Republican party, won as senator with 71 percent; and Byron L. Dorgan, a Democrat of progressive bent who had endorsed Kennedy for the Democratic presidential nomination, was elected as that state's lone House member with 57 percent of the vote. In South Dakota, Carter dropped 17 percent, from 49 percent in 1976 to 32 percent in 1980. One of the two South Dakota House seats went to Representative Thomas Daschle, who has a liberally oriented record but a conservative personal style; he won 66 to 34 percent.

Those who see a sweeping conservative trend outside the South have not studied the votes carefully. The American public voted against inflation and for candidates they felt would address our problems more effectively. Ideology appears to have been a secondary consideration for most voters.

I do not suggest that the secondary consideration should be ignored. One of the nation's most thoughtful Democrats, Milton Katz, who succeeded Averill Harriman as the administrator of the Marshall Plan in Europe and who for many years headed the international legal studies program at Harvard, suggests that the Democratic party has become skewed. He argues that the party of Franklin Roosevelt and Harry Truman stressed the creation of a just and more equitable society and, at the same time, stressed productivity and growth. Katz believes that, starting with Lyndon Johnson, while the stress on justice has continued, there has been a diminishing concern for the other part of the equation. "And unless there is growth in productivity, there is nothing additional to share with the most needy in our society," he points out.[3] This weakness of the Democratic party in recent years did cost the party votes.

This reality does not suggest that Democrats should abandon their role as the champions of those who face great need. If it ceases to be the advocate for social justice, the Democratic party might as well forget politics, for it will have lost its reason for existence. But justice must be combined with healthy growth. And a society that is fairer to all can also be a society that places greater stress on quality of performance.

Voters rarely frame questions in philosophical terms, and most did not in 1980. They asked practical questions about inflation and unemployment and energy and leadership. The year 1980 did not begin the millennium for the Republican party, unless the Democrats hand them the future.

CHAPTER TWO

A Lesson from History

W infield Scott Hancock is one of the least remembered Democratic candidates for president, as well he should be. He ran against James A. Garfield in 1880. A general with little knowledge of the issues, Hancock ran a colorless campaign with no emphasis on problems confronting the nation. The Cincinnati Democratic convention that nominated Hancock had sought someone who had offended no one. They got what they were looking for — and lost the election.

Alton B. Parker is another name few will recall. Democrats nominated Parker in 1904 to oppose Theodore Roosevelt, portraying him less than accurately as a conservative candidate, in an effort to take votes away from Teddy. The plan backfired and Theodore Roosevelt won overwhelmingly.

Political parties or candidates without ideas, who simply tell the electorate, "We can do the job better," rarely win. There are exceptions. General Dwight D. Eisenhower was such an exception, a national hero who had the public's confidence. He will probably be judged by future historians more kindly than by the current generation of observers, though not as kindly as by the American people of his time. But Eisenhower was an exception to the rule. A "me-too" candidate, who pledges nothing substantially different than the incumbent, simply that he or she can do the job better, generally loses.

There is a danger for candidates in the next election — any next election — to repeat the formula that brought victory to others in the last election. So the me-too candidate is born. Me-tooism is a disease that has afflicted a variety of candidates through the years. The disease is usually fatal. If the afflicted candidate does survive the election, he or she rarely serves well once elected, for those who have the malady don't know what to do once elected. Those Democrats who advise the party simply to imitate the Republicans offer doomed counsel.

The me-too illness is now compounded by the dramatic rise in public-opinion polling and the spectacle of public officials following the implications of polls, regardless of national need. This craven idolatry of the golden calf of our generation makes the actions of ancient Aaron and his followers appear statesmanlike.

No candidate and no political party can ignore public opinion. Still, the purpose of elections is to choose men and women who will lead in meeting national (or local) needs, not follow blindly the shifts of public opinion item by item, issue by issue.

Jimmy Carter's presidency is a classic example of too careful attention to public-opinion polls. Much about the Carter presidency has not been adequately appreciated — particularly the Middle East agreement hammered out at Camp David — but his failure to lead on some of the basic domestic economic problems resulted, in no small part, from much too great a reliance on polling.

In July 1979 I wrote for the weekly newspaper column in my district:

> The Carter administration, to much too great a degree, has been determining policy by studying national polls rather than national needs. That does not result in effective leadership.
>
> If the media reports are correct, the Carter decision to have a Camp David summit, and to fire some cabinet members after asking all to submit resignations, grew out of recommendations made by Carter's pollster.
>
> Two days after his resignation, Secretary of the Treasury Michael Blumenthal spoke in Chicago, generally supportive of the President's fiscal policies, but he carefully worked in a criticism of "timid politicians and mindless pollsters."
>
> While this particular criticism is directed at the President and Pat Caddell, the same criticism can be leveled at much of Congress. We are collectively holding our finger to the wind to learn the latest direction in public opinion. Then we act, or decline to act.
>
> The nation is ill served by that shaky type of performance.
>
> In a recent issue of *Foreign Affairs*, former Sen. J. William Fulbright speaks about this problem, and although he is writing of Congress, his words apply with equal validity to the presidency:

> Our elected representatives . . . study and analyze public attitudes by sophisticated new techniques, but their purpose has little to do with leadership. . . . Their purpose, it seems, is to discover what people want and fear and dislike, and then to identify themselves with those sentiments. They seek to discover which issues can be safely emphasized and which are more prudently avoided. This approach to politics is the opposite of leadership; it is followership, for purposes of self-advancement . . .

The President could extricate himself from the problem by stopping all poll-taking and simply ask himself two basic questions: What are the most pressing needs of this country? How can we in government help to meet those needs?

Interestingly, in the area where the President relies least on polling for establishing policy — foreign affairs — in that area he has done best. Where he is weak — domestic policy — he relies heavily on the polls.

I doubt that the President will move away from his reliance on polling and Congress will have an equally hard time extricating itself from the polling quicksand, because members of the House and Senate have discovered that polling breeds success — if you measure success by winning elections. But it does not breed quality leadership. And, unfortunately, I could cite some "good" examples.

We need people — in the executive branch and in Congress — who are willing to sail against the winds of public opinion, who are willing to make the tough decisions this nation needs.

Whether or not President Carter has it within himself to become an effective leader is difficult to know. He is a decent man with fundamentally good instincts, but that does not automatically translate into leadership.

Whatever leadership potential he has is being impaired by those who hand him endless reams of polling statistics.

We yearn for effective leadership, and polls will not provide it.

Within six months of Carter's taking office, political observer Henry Fairlie wrote prophetically that if Carter continued his policy of following polls to set policy "he is headed for an electoral disaster. . . . If Caddell has his way, there will be no Jimmy Carter visible at the next election; and he will lose." He added these significant words: "Politics is meant to create; it is not meant merely to manipulate."[1]

The night of the Wisconsin presidential primary, April 1, 1980, the national television spokesman for the Carter cause in Milwaukee was, appropriately, Pat Caddell. It marked the first time in the nation's history that a pollster served as spokesman for a president on an election night. And on November 4, 1980, President Carter conceded defeat, even before ballot boxes were closed on the West Coast, on the basis of "exit polls," — measurements taken during the election day by television networks of the voting in a few key districts, and which are announced as soon as the polls close.

Patrick Caddell is an excellent pollster. But polls should be used for limited functions and not for establishing public policy.

In the *Federalist Papers,* "Publius" (either James Madison or Alexander Hamilton) noted that the people need "a safeguard against the tyranny of their own passions."[2] That is as true today as it was then.

If the Democratic party decides its course on the basis of public-opinion polls, it is destined to produce candidates of the caliber of Winfield Scott Hancock, and it will fail in its most basic function: providing constructive policies to meet the nation's needs.

Can you imagine Hubert Humphrey taking a poll on how he should vote on a civil-rights bill? Or Harry Truman taking a poll on almost anything before making a decision? I do not suggest that the party ignore public opinion; there is little danger that candidates or a political party will do that. The danger is the opposite extreme.

Almost two thousand years ago, the historian and biographer Plutarch wrote: "For this is indeed the true condition of men in public life, who, to gain the vain title of being the people's leaders and governors, are content to make themselves the slaves and followers of all the people's humors and caprices. . . . These men, steered, as I may say, by popular applause, though they bear the name of governors, are in reality the mere underlings of the multitude. . . . As Phocion answered King Antipater, who sought his approbation of some unworthy action, 'I cannot be your flatterer and your friend,' so these men should answer the people, 'I cannot govern and obey you.' "[3]

Winston Churchill thoughtfully observed: "Nothing is more dangerous than to live in the temperamental atmosphere of a Gallup poll, always taking one's pulse and taking one's political tempera-ture. . . . There is only one duty, only one safe course, and that is to try to be right and not to fear to do or to say what you believe to be right."[4]

CHAPTER THREE

Needed: A Sense of Concern

W hat people seek from government, and from a political party, among other things, is the sense that there is understanding and concern about "my" problems, and that is universally true whether the person is the president of General Motors or a welfare recipient in Detroit. Sensing that those who govern — or hope to govern — have a concern about "my" problems provides hope, and we are sustained by hope almost as much as by food and water. Somehow in 1980 the Democratic party failed to convey that sense of concern and hope to people who should be our advocates. Such hope is not entirely self-centered, though at times it comes close to that. There is a willingness to help others, but a political party cannot be successful and convey the impression of aid to others without relating it in some way to "my" problems.

There is some truth to the comment of my colleague from North Carolina, Representative Charles Rose: "We have built an excess in expectation of what government can do."[1] There are places where government action is needed and needed badly. But when candidates and public officials overpromise and underproduce, we invite — and deserve — political retribution. Part of the problem of both political parties is not simply that the public believes we have ignored people's problems, but they sense political dialogue has led to preelection concern and postelection indifference.

The Democratic party has slipped in part because of its success. The programs have succeeded well enough so that people who have been helped by government have increased their income, moved to the suburbs (mentally, if not physically), and now vote Republican with their neighbors. Not only does voting Republican become socially more acceptable, but as a person's income goes up it becomes easier to find flaws in the expenditures of public funds and reasons why those funds should stay in "my" pocket rather than go to the federal government for distribution to others. Winston Churchill often told the story of the man who risked his life to save a drowning child. When he brought the child to his mother, she asked in outrage, "Where's Johnny's cap?" The Democratic party is in a similar situation with many people.

The rewriting of history by Republican speechmakers is anything but accurate. The programs that emerged from Franklin Roosevelt and the succeeding Democratic presidents for the most part succeeded in lifting the lot of the poor and in helping average Americans achieve economic progress most of their parents never dreamed possible. The percentage of Americans below the poverty level is at a record low. And those who complain about government programs today generally do so from homes with wall-to-wall carpeting, air conditioning, and color television. If Republicans want to suggest that some of the Democratic initiatives were flawed, there would be no dispute. Where a program is flawed, it should be corrected; where it is unneeded, abandon it.

Part of the problem, however, is related to the nature of news. When programs go well, they do not make the news. If foreign aid today results in five hundred thousand young people in North Africa on the brink of starvation receiving a daily glass of milk, it will not make the news. But an abuse of foreign aid — or any program — will make the news. If the only things people read and hear and see about governmental action are the abuses, understandably they will oppose the programs. Tests show that those who watch television regularly have a greatly exaggerated view of the extent of the crime problem. That is hardly a surprise. And those who see only the bad side of government programs in the news regularly have a similarly distorted picture. On balance, government programs of the last four decades have achieved remarkable progress for the nation — and that news will startle some. Yet that is the reality.

However, a party should not be supported simply on the basis of its past policies. People ask, "What will you do for me in the future?" And they are increasingly willing to ask, "What will you do for the country in the future?" There is a growing recognition that what is good for the nation as a whole should be supported even if it involves some personal sacrifice. There may be skeptics who doubt that last sentence, but I have seen the evidence over and over again in my years in public life. People are willing to sacrifice if they feel that others are being asked to make a similar sacrifice and if their sacrifice helps to meet a genuine need. If that were not true, how would a school bond issue ever pass? The citizens of this country will respond affirmatively when provided the right kind of leadership. Americans yearn for firm, effective leadership. That is one of Ronald Reagan's strengths. His leadership, however, also happens to be leading in the wrong direction; but that is less clear to most people. And that wrong direction is not simply that the president has called for a redistribution of wealth, with more for the top few and less for the bottom many; it is leading in the wrong direction in appealing too much to our sense of self-centeredness. We do not need that; it is enough a part of all of us. We need appeals to our better instincts, not our worse. The "look out for number one" attitude will always be present to some degree, but it has taken a stronger hold on our society than is healthy. And ironically, to the extent that our sense of community breaks down, selfishness becomes self-defeating, shortsighted, and stupid. The Reagan approach inevitably will increase discussions that pit economic class against economic class. Those realities are present in any society, but as differences grow and opportunities to bridge them diminish, there is more heat and hatred and momentum in the dialogue. Americans want to feel that the concerns of *all* citizens have been weighed carefully as decisions are made, and they are starting to understand that the Reagan approach does not do that.

But Democrats must do more to express a breadth of concern.

In my district it is widely known that I oppose a constitutional amendment that would ban abortion, but it is not as widely known that I consider abortion a tragic option that ought to be used rarely and that I believe government and the private sectors, working together, should find constructive alternatives to abortion. I have conveyed my concerns less effectively than I should. I should be telling business leaders in my district that the black-lung program I helped push through is not simply a union program for former coal miners and their widows, but brings millions of dollars to the economy of southern Illinois.

Let me give you an illustration of something I did well. When New York City first faced its potential bankruptcy difficulties and needed federal assistance, my mail was overwhelmingly against any help. Over and over I heard: "Why should we in rural southern Illinois help New York City?" I wrote to the banks in my district and asked how many of them had New York City bonds. About half of the banks replied and I learned that more than one-third of these financial institutions in southern Illinois had sizable investments in the high-interest yield bonds of New York City. I was able to show the people of my district that we could be hurt very directly if New York City defaulted on her bonds. Rural America must understand that it has a stake in urban America, and urban America must understand more fully its stake in rural problems.

The Democratic party must listen more effectively. *Effectively* is the right word. For example, too many witnesses before congressional committees, which until recently Democrats controlled in both Houses, have gone out of their way to prepare testimony, fly to Washington, and find one senator or one House member half listening to the testimony. They go away feeling that it would have been as useful to give the same testimony in the middle of a Kansas wheat field.

Black and Hispanic Americans still feel that the Democratic party is their best hope; but as their income level climbs, that base can erode. The unskilled and untrained continue to look to the Democratic party as their champion. Democrats cannot give up that role, but the party also needs to hold these voters once they become skilled and trained.

Middle-income parents who must struggle to get children through college should sense Democratic concern. Labor-union members should feel Democrats listen not only to their leaders, but to their membership as well. Industrial leaders should understand the party's concerns for industrial safety, but they should understand equally as firmly that Democrats do not favor unnecessary regulation and want to encourage business growth and development. Senior citizens should sense clearly that the Democratic party understands their frustrations and is trying to help. The average age of veterans is climbing, and that means more health problems. They should know that the party of Andrew Jackson wants the finest care for them in veterans hospitals and no slackening of veterans' benefits. Women must understand that Democrats favor assistance where necessary to those who choose to work at home while raising a family and equal pay and opportunity for those who choose work opportunities in the job market. People interested in improvement of the quality of education and the quality of manufactured products and the quality of life generally should feel that the Democratic party is their champion. Young people who want to own a farm someday should feel that Democrats understand their dilemma and want to help them implement their dream.

The list could go on and on — and it must. There are broad concerns of huge groups of people such as those just mentioned, but there are much smaller groups we too easily overlook. Japanese-Americans are a numerically small group, but their special sensitivity to what happened to them during World War II, when without cause or justification they were herded into camps away from the West Coast, is a justified one. The Latter-Day Saints (Mormons) took a strong stand against the racetrack basing mode of the MX missile —a shell-game scheme for hiding missiles among a host of empty shells, a scheme which many military leaders have denounced privately and many who are retired have laughed at publicly, and which would have taken huge chunks of land in Utah and Nevada. President Reagan properly dropped the project, but Mormons should know that some of us who are Democrats led the fight against the MX basing mode for several years, greatly influencing the president's decision. In a few states, the Mormons carry great weight, but their smaller numbers in many states are too easily overlooked. Christian Scientists are not a large group in most congressional districts, but they have special concerns about health legislation as it touches on their religious beliefs. Armenian-Americans are not huge in number, but they have a rich heritage and a history of persecution. Their special legislative wants are almost nonexistent, but they are sensitive to those who show an awareness of their special heritage. The list continues indefinitely, for diversity is what this nation represents. The Democratic party must continue its historic role of serving as the catalyst for hope to that great diversity.

There must be no slackening of concern. Franklin D. Roosevelt spoke for more than his generation when he said that the measure of a healthy society is its response to the most vulnerable. However, the concern must be — and I believe generally is — for all people. That includes middle-income America. When a paraplegic gets an education and develops skills, thanks to a Democratically launched initiative, and his or her annual income climbs to over $25,000, that person should not feel he or she is no longer the concern of the Democratic party.

Some suggest that to appeal to middle America the party should denounce welfare and food stamps and foreign aid. It is an easy way to get votes. But it is also demagogic and irresponsible. A better way — a responsible way — is to acknowledge that any program can be improved, but to tell the truth about the myths. Democrats should let business people know that foreign economic assistance helps American businesses; political leaders must help the public understand that food stamps have dramatically reduced malnutrition in our country while helping the elderly and farmers and grocery stores; and the party must demonstrate to voters that money spent educating the handicapped saves money that would otherwise be used for their support.

A few years ago I attended a foundation-sponsored think-tank session at Zion Beach State Park on Lake Michigan, north of Chicago. An author and state-university professor at the meeting commented, "I guess I'm like most people. I'm tired of seeing my money going constantly to help the poor."

I asked him how he had arrived at the conference. He had flown into O'Hare Airport, he said. I asked him if that tax-supported airport was designed primarily to help the poor. From O'Hare he came by interstate highway to the meeting. I observed that most of those I see on the subsidized interstate highways are not the poor. The beautiful lodge at the state park where we were staying — built with tax money — did not house any poor. And then I noted that the tax-supported state university at which he teaches had a disproportionately high percentage of students from middle- and upper-income families. I doubt that I convinced him. But this bright and articulate leader had accepted without much reflection the common view that most of his tax money was going to help the poor. The truth becomes warped.

The Democratic party has a story to tell of service and concern for all. The party should develop effective ways of showing what we have done to cut red tape, to help business, to encourage farmers and dentists and coal miners and car dealers at the same time that we help the poor and the oppressed.

Twenty physicians who are Democrats (some may say I have suggested the impossible already) could send a letter to every other physician in the country saying basically: "Before Medicare became a reality the American Medical Association fought it strenuously. Over the combined opposition of the AMA and the Republican party it was enacted. It's not perfect, but it has been a godsend to millions of this nation's senior citizens and it has done no harm to the private practice of medicine. We're interested in your comments on how we can improve Medicare, reduce some of the paperwork, and meet the medical needs in this nation that our present system does not meet." Make those responses available to all members of the House and Senate. Would this tactic get any votes? Perhaps not; but it would produce some good ideas, soften some attitudes, and show some people who contribute immensely to the welfare of the nation that Democrats are concerned and are listening to them. *And the party must listen.*

At a dinner I attended recently I talked wtih F. Eugene Purcell, a senior vice president of Lone Star Industries, Inc. He told me: "I'm a Democrat and outspoken and open about it. But I don't see my party telling business leaders what Democrats have contributed to business stability and growth. I don't see my party leaders paying much attention to business except when it comes to fund-raising time." Democrats should and must communicate — not only because it will mean votes, but also because it can help the party govern more effectively when in power.

Labor leaders tell a similar story. They feel taken for granted. Democrats *assume* their support. Yet they feel ignored. There needs to be more frank give-and-take between Democratic officials and labor leaders, talking over what can and cannot be done — and listening to their sense of priorities. A party that ignores labor leaders and working men and women eventually will be ignored itself. And while labor leaders feel lack of attention, many rank-and-file members are out-and-out alienated. I remember campaigning at plant gates in 1968 — plants organized by progressive unions — and seeing scores of "Wallace for President" buttons on the shirts of the workers. In

1980 there was a somewhat smaller display of Reagan buttons and a more pronounced display of Reagan votes.

Part of the problem is simply cynicism toward all government, an outgrowth of Vietnam, Watergate, and Abscam, for which the Democrats share responsibility. But it is more than that. What our fellow citizens yearn for is firm, dedicated leadership that displays genuine concern for their interests. They do not expect complete agreement, and they do not want to hear a fawning, patronizing, uncertain voice from their party leadership. But they will vote for, and support when elected, a political party's leadership that listens to them and speaks with a compassionate and certain voice.

CHAPTER FOUR

Balanced Budgets and Inflation

"To be a liberal does not mean you favor wasting money," one of this nation's greatest senators, Paul H. Douglas, used to say.

There is much in the record of Democrats "to which we can point with pride," as do the campaign orators, but in the area of fiscal policy the Democratic record has had some shortcomings.

But so have the Republicans! And there is no clearer illustration than the Ronald Reagan tax package, which he somehow wrapped in the label "conservative," though its contents were anything but conservative. For that mammoth tax cut means that a balanced budget will be impossible to achieve. The Reagan economic package assures interest rates higher than they should be into the foreseeable future, assuming the Federal Reserve Board maintains stability of the money supply. And now the president who campaigned in every state proclaiming the virtues of a balanced budget is responsible for record-breaking deficits.

After the Reagan tax cut passed Congress and before the president signed it into law, the respected *Washington Post* financial columnist Hobart Rowen wrote:

> In the past several days, bond prices have plunged and interest rates have soared. Two-year Treasury notes, auctioned July 22, hit an all-time record yield of 15.92 percent, and the Dow Jones Municpal Bond Index touched a peak of 12.25 percent. All other interest rates were at, or on the edge of, records.
>
> What this dismal picture suggests is that the financial markets have no more confidence in the beneficial effects of the Reagan program, now that it is about to become law, than they had while it was being debated.[1]

The Democratic record on the issue of a balanced budget has not been good, but now the Republican record becomes worse. Interest payments are a good illustration of the problem the nation faces.

	1950	1960	1970	1980	1981*	1982*
Interest on debt (billions)	$5.7	$8.3	$18.3	$64.5	$95.3	$98.1
Per capita (dollars)	$37	$46	$89	$285	$415	$427

Estimated by Congressional Budget Office

An increasing percentage of the federal tax dollar is going for interest, and that does not make sense, whether you are a liberal or a conservative, a Democrat or a Republican. In 1967, 8.5 percent of the federal government's outlay went for interest, and in 1981 it will be at least 14.2 percent. If for fiscal year 1981 we could have spent $84 billion on interest rather than $94 billion, we could have used that extra $10 billion in ways that would have enriched the nation immensely. (For example: $5 billion to create 750,000 jobs for people who are not working; $3 billion toward encouraging capital formation; $1.3 billion to include dentures, hearing aids, and eyeglasses under Medicare; $700 million to significantly improve federal assistance for education for the handicapped.) The largest single expenditure by the federal government is now for Social Security and related payments; the second largest is defense; the third is interest. *For fiscal year 1981 we spent more for interest than we spent for higher education, energy, agriculture, foreign aid, pollution control, health research, veterans' benefits, and the FBI combined.*

That huge expenditure for interest is not turned around overnight. Had we followed a policy of greater fiscal prudence ten years ago or twenty years ago, we would not have the high interest rates we have today, nor the heavy interest payments that distort the federal expenditure. A common desire for a wise expenditure of funds is one reason for moving away from year-after-year deficits.

A second reason is inflation.

Federal deficits are not the sole cause of inflation that many make them out to be, but they are a significant factor. Some point to oil prices or world grain shortages as causes for inflation — and they are important factors — but nations much more heavily dependent on imported oil and imported grain (such as Japan, West Germany, Switzerland, and the Netherlands) have significantly smaller inflation rates. As a general rule, it is true that nations operating with both fiscal and monetary prudence have low rates of inflation.

Let me outline in question-and-answer format the realities, as I see them, of federal deficits and inflation.

How are federal deficits inflationary?

They are inflationary in two ways. First, the federal government must go into the money market to cover the indebtedness. In many ways the money market is like the market for tomatoes or wheat or anything else: the law of supply and demand prevails. Given a constant supply and increased demand, money costs more — interest rates go up. Higher interest rates are a major cause of inflation. Second, if the federal intrusion into the money market causes too much pain, the Federal Reserve Board increases the supply (prints more money) and that too is inflationary.

The Democratic party must seek areas that unite broad segments of the party and bring outsiders into the fold. One of these issues is low interest rates. My colleagues in Congress who are "boll weevils" — southern Democrats who generally support Reagan economic programs — oppose high interest rates, as do the legislators from New York and Massachusetts. Harry Truman used to say that, if you rose from the grave and wondered which party was in power, ask about interest rates. If they're high, the Republicans are in power, and if they're low, the Democrats are. Interest rates during the Carter years seemed to contradict the Truman dictum, but the average rate during the Reagan years is likely to make the Carter years look much better.

Four days before the Reagan administration took office, former Federal Reserve Board Chairman Arthur Burns and a distinguished group of economic leaders of the nation, including three former secretaries of the Treasury, sent a statement on inflation to all members of Congress. Among its warnings: "The new recession, if it occurs, will in large part be a product of the extraordinary levels attained by interest rates."[2] Interest rates have climbed significantly since then.

Some form of credit control, such as requiring 20 percent down on all items costing above $400, could moderate interest rates. Truman used that mechanism successfully, but combined it with sound fiscal and tax policy. It is unlikely that the Reagan administration will use credit controls, and it is even more clear that balanced budgets will not be in the picture. Continued large deficits will mean high interest rates.

Should there never be deficits?

When employment takes a dip, when the economy becomes sluggish, there almost inevitably is a deficit. One percent unemployment costs the federal government roughly $22 billion. When we have high unemployment, we should plan on modest deficits. Our difficulty is that what is needed in times of recession has become habitual. We will soon mark only one year out of twenty-three when we have not had a deficit.

Is defense spending inflationary?

Any spending that causes deficits tends to be inflationary. Defense-minded people blame the deficit on social programs and social-minded people blame the deficit on defense programs, and both are partially right and partially wrong.

There are some factors, however, that make defense spending more inflationary than other spending, among them the fact that a substantial percentage of our research talent, compared to that of West Germany and Japan, is in defense-oriented work. And while there are sometimes benefits in nonmilitary fields (aerospace and computers are two examples from military research), generally there are no civilian applications.

Poorly programed defense spending can have major inflationary pressures and that is where we are headed as I write this. At the beginning of the Korean War Harry Truman asked for an increase in taxes, and at the end of the war inflation was actually less than at the beginning. One of the reasons for inflation today is that, between 1965 and 1970, defense expenditures went up $26.9 billion, and for understandable political reasons Lyndon Johnson did not ask for a tax increase. President Reagan asked for a defense-spending increase from 1981 to 1986 of $197 billion. Even allowing for substantial inflation, that is more than a threefold increase over the growth in spending during the Vietnam period — and Reagan is getting a substantial tax cut. That is a recipe for more inflation. The *Chicago Tribune* noted editorially: "The country cannot slash tax rates and engage in a huge military buildup at the same time without running either high rates of inflation or high rates of interest, or both."[3]

Buckminster Fuller, one of the most creative minds of the nation, puts the problem this way: "The military has prior access to the high performance capabilities of the economy, the best of the instruments, the most beautiful production tools. Whatever it may be, military has prior access. When you have priority, you have to have antipriority. Who has to do with the leftovers? And it always has been the home front. That really has been the attitude of all government since Malthus's time, with humanity in general not knowing this." Fuller also says that if production could be retooled from "weaponry to . . . livingry, within ten years all humanity [could] enjoy the highest standard of living anybody has every known."[4]

Should we follow the suggestion of those who would limit federal expenditures to a percentage of the gross national product (GNP)?

No. When national income (gross national product) dips, the federal government should spend more. When national income rises and we have high employment, federal expenditure should taper off. To limit federal expenditures to a percentage of the gross national product would be to accomplish precisely the opposite. Conservative columnist George Will is among those who have pointed out the folly of such an approach. The federal government should be a force for stability in the economic roller coaster, contrary to the Reagan rhetoric, which views government as the great evil in the economic picture. Limiting to a percentage of GNP would, in the "down" years, put the squeeze on the least articulate in our society: the poor. West Germany and Japan and other nations provide clear examples that prosperity and greater economic justice can both occur. We already had some problems in this respect before the Reagan economic package; now they are worse. The 1981 *World Development Report* published by the World Bank has the weakness of using data several years old, but it shows that of the eighteen industrialized nations, only France gives the lowest 20 percent of its population a smaller percentage of the nation's gross national product than does the United States.[5]

This means that we already have an income-distribution problem, aggravated substantially by the Reagan program. Suggestions to tie federal expenditures to GNP will worsen the equity problem and intensify both the boom and bust periods, and that's not good economic sense.

Don't we simply owe the federal debt to ourselves?

There are a number of things wrong with that assumption, including two major flaws. First, in today's world those who buy bonds live in places like Saudi Arabia, Kuwait, and Singapore, as well as Creal Springs, Illinois, and Tarpon Springs, Florida. That helps our balance of payments but reduces our control of the situation. Second, payment of interest by the government is a regressive redistribution factor. The income to pay for the interest comes from all income levels, but those who buy and hold the bonds and benefit directly tend to be in the upper-income brackets. Government indebtedness complicates the wealth-distribution problem in the United States.

But don't such countries as Japan and West Germany also have deficits?

Sometimes they do. But our national debt is approximately 38.2 percent of our GNP, Japan's is 22.3 percent, and West Germany's 13.8 percent. And even that gives a distorted figure, for state and local government indebtedness is not calculated in these totals, and in the United States, state and local indebtedness is much greater than in Japan and West Germany.

But isn't inflation inevitable? And does it really do any harm?

We have had long periods of history in our country with virtually no inflation. For example, from 1955 to 1965 inflation averaged 1.6 percent a year.

As to its harm, hundreds of examples could be cited. A man I talked to recently invested wisely during his working years so that he could have $9,600 a year to live on — which he felt could make his retirement years almost golden. Ten years after retirement he finds this sum is worth half what it once was. He is experiencing real difficulties simply meeting his day-to-day living expenses and his above-average medically related bills. That's one small example.

If the inflation rate were 7 percent a year — and that now looks attractive — in ten years prices virtually double, in twenty years almost quadruple, and in thirty years increase by a factor of almost eight. In thirty years a dollar would be worth thirteen cents, an $8,000 car would cost $61,000. That kind of inflation would mean a drastic altering of our thrift institutions; it would devastate the life-insurance industry, which is so important to many American families and — not so incidentally — to the bond market. (Most Americans would be amazed at how many of their local projects have been financed by life-insurance companies.) Even the most casual study of the impact of inflation shows it to be a monster that can devour our economic base. If that happens, can our freedom itself survive? The lesson of history is clear, as a Japanese publication concludes: "Inflation is the foe of freedom."[6]

If deficits are not the answer, don't we have to make massive cuts in the social programs Democrats have traditionally believed in?

That is one option, but not one I prefer. That is the option chosen by the Reagan administration. The Reagan budget cuts primarily affect the poor. Never before in United States history have we had such a conscious, clear-cut program of cutting back on benefits for the poor and elderly and increasing the benefits for those of upper incomes. William Niskanen, a member of President Reagan's Council of Economic Advisers, has defended these priorities: "A misconception about the Reagan economic policy is that it is pro wealthy people, that it has adopted a rather simple, crude version of trickle-down economics in which somehow if you give enough money to wealthy people, it gets to somebody else. A more appropriate characterization of Reagan economic policy is that we want to improve the opportunity to become wealthy. . . . In general that serves the interests of all of us."[7] There are few Democrats who want to deny people the opportunity to become wealthy — but most Democrats and most Americans do not want to do it on the backs of those who can least afford it.

Interestingly, the programs espoused by Democrats since Franklin Roosevelt's day have permitted more people to enter the ranks of the wealthy than have Republican programs. Where there are efforts that emphasize both improved distribution and improved productivity, increased wealth is possible. These Democratic programs are regularly denounced by most of those who have accumulated wealth under them — denounced all the way to the bank.

Other options include stability, rather than growth, in the defense budget, assuming international tensions make that possible; or prudently reducing the tax rate. The mix the Reagan administration has chosen is to cut programs for the poor and elderly, increase the defense budget, and substantially lower taxes. It is a mix that invites major social as well as economic problems. Taxes, as a percent of national income, are lower in the United States than in almost all of the industrial countries. I am not advocating higher taxes, but much of what I read and hear must seem strange to visitors from other countries. The total cost of government as a percentage of GNP is lower in the United States than in any industrial nation other than Japan. And in Japan, defense takes less than 1 percent of the GNP, while in the United States it takes 6 percent; in Japan, industries assume the responsibility for what would be the equivalent of our Social Security program. The total (federal, state, and local) burden of government in the United States is 31 percent of our GNP, compared to 42 percent in West Germany for one example. All the major European countries are over 40 percent.

The great growth in taxes over the last two decades has been in state and local government rather than the federal government. The great cause of growth at that level — education — is tapering off because of population shifts. Although the public image of the federal government is of "a mushrooming bureaucracy" (to use an overworked phrase), in fact, the numbers of federal workers per 100,000 people declined between 1960 and 1980. One of the things Jimmy Carter did not get credit for from the public was a reduction in the total number of federal employees by more than 55,000 from the day he took office until the day he left. In 1960 the federal government purchased 11 percent of the national economy's output, but by 1980 that had dropped to 8 percent.

In 1949, 13.9 out of every thousand Americans worked for the federal government; in 1979, 12.7. In 1950, 4.2 million people worked for state and local governments; in 1979, 13.1 million. In 1950, state and local government employees represented 67 percent of the government work force; in 1979, 82 percent. Reversing that, federal employees represented 33 percent of government employees in 1950, 18 percent in 1979.

Are Democrats responsible for high inflation?

Democrats bear a share of the blame, but Republican administrations have been no better in fiscal matters than Democratic administrations. In Congress — prior to the Reagan administration — most of the Republican moves to bring order to our fiscal house had been grandstanding efforts, with an eye to the camera rather than the economy. There have been exceptions, the most notable being those of Senator Henry Bellmon, a recently retired Republican senator from Oklahoma who worked closely with Senator Edmund Muskie on budgetary matters. Bellmon probed the basic questions as few others have. He called for a study, for example, of what the security needs of the nation really are and how we can coordinate foreign policy and defense policy more effectively.

The budgetary process now followed by Congress was initiated by Democrats. Without this new budgetary restraint, we would be in much worse shape than we now are.

What about Social Security? Is Reagan right? Are the funds in bad shape?

There is a Social Security problem, but we do not need an assault on senior citizens to solve it. If the original Reagan proposal had been approved, those retiring in 1982 at the age of sixty-two would have had their Social Security income cut an average of one-third, and by 1987 cut even more than one-third. Those retiring at sixty-five would not have been reduced in 1982, but would have been cut an average of 4 percent in 1987. The Reagan proposal also would have changed Social Security eligibility so that people would have to have worked seven and a half years out of the last ten to be eligible for Social Security, a real problem in areas of high unemployment, a particular problem for people who are in the above-fifty-five age group. This is but one of a series of assaults the Reagan administration proposed on the elderly, most of which fortunately were rejected by Congress.

What should be done? There are three Social Security trust funds: the retirement fund, the Medicare fund, and the disability fund. The retirement fund is the only one with an immediate problem, caused by inflation no one ever expected, which sent expenditures way up, and caused by high unemployment, which brought income down. A jobs program, as outlined in Chapter Five, requiring those who get jobs to pay Social Security, would help solve the problem. Correcting the index by which cost-of-living increases are measured would assist significantly. This could be done by using a separate index for the elderly, or by using the current index but putting housing on a rental-equivalency basis rather than purchase basis, as the Reagan administration apparently will now do. There is increasing talk about deregulating natural gas, and if the Reagan administration gets its way on that, there should be a windfall tax on the major companies (not the royalty owners and small producers) with perhaps one-third of that windfall tax designated for the Social Security retirement fund; that would solve the problem, though Reagan has pledged opposition to such an approach. Senator William Proxmire says that the trust funds are not being managed in such a way as to draw maximum interest, and the 8.3 percent average interest they now draw tends to confirm his charge. It could be that simply managing the three trust funds better so that they earn more interest will alleviate the Social Security problem, though that does not solve the federal treasury part of it. The *Washington Post* reports the 1982 shortfall will be $5 to $7 billion, and when you consider that the tax-cut bill signed by President Reagan slashed taxes $750 billion over a five-year period, we ought to be able to find the Social Security shortfall without devastating the retirement hopes of the elderly.[8]

In addition to reducing budget deficits, what are some other ways we can deal with inflation?

In general, we need some steady policies that recognize that inflation cannot be cured overnight, that there are no painless remedies, and that it will take a series of actions to reduce inflation, not one, single dramatic gesture. In 1979 a bipartisan Task Force on Inflation of the House Budget Committee issued a report that, among other things, made these recommendations which I have summarized:

1. The Federal Reserve Board should generally follow a steady path on monetary policy. Some flexibility is needed, but not much.

2. Caution is in order on tax cuts, and when tax cuts come they should encourage savings and capital formation. Tax cuts that simply increase demand add to inflation. And tax cuts add to deficits.

3. The president should be given standby authority to create public-service jobs, targeted to areas of high unemployment. (See Chapter Five.)

4. Legitimate defense needs have to be met, but caution is in order before huge increases are accepted. Part of the nation's security is a healthy economy. (See Chapter Thirteen.)

5. Keep the credit-allocation authority the president and the Federal Reserve Board now jointly have. There may be times when it is much wiser to use credit controls, rather than high interest rates, to slow the economy.

6. Resist further efforts to index tax rates or index anything else. Indexing is in and of itself inflationary. Both Japan and Germany forbid cost-of-living provisions in contracts. (Unfortunately, we are

moving toward more and more indexation — including the tax rates — and that is inflationary.)*

7. Reduce oil imports. (See Chapter Twelve.)

8. Strengthen our exports.

9. Study the increasing concentration of economic power in the hands of fewer and fewer corporations. This deserves much more serious attention than it has received. (Unfortunately, the policies of the Reagan administration are accelerating the process of merger and concentration. In their view, big government is bad, but big business is good. In fact, both have their dangers, including the practical one of rigidity and inflexibility. Big business can have the added problem of reducing competition. A free-enterprise system is premised on competition, and factors that inhibit the competitive forces, such as the dominance of one corporation in a field, do not serve the nation's economy well.)

10. A youth differential is needed in our minimum wage. When minimum wages go up, youth unemployment also goes up. We need to give young people a chance for employment, and the West European experience with a youth differential indicates that young workers are not substituted for older workers. (It's a little like the old arguments on fair-employment practices: if you put blacks to work, whites will be forced out of jobs. We now know that when we expand the opportunity to work, everyone benefits. Congressman Henry Reuss of Wisconsin has suggested as a compromise to the controversial youth-differential proposal that it be tried in a limited number of states or for a limited time period.)

11. Regulations should be reduced. Most regulations must be kept, but every study suggests that we are overregulated, adding to our productivity problems. The Inflation Task Force calls many regulations "too detailed, too cumbersome, lacking in common sense, and totally uncoordinated."[9] They change so rapidly that industries don't know where they stand. Regulatory bodies also cause needless, costly, excessive delays. (For all the ills attributed to regulation, few would want drugs sold unregulated, or no air pollution or water pollution controls, or total abolition of regulations in almost any area. But more common sense must be exercised.)

*Comments in parentheses in these fifteen points are the author's, not part of the original report.

12. Agricultural programs that set aside land to reduce grain production should become a part of history. Paying farmers not to produce makes no more sense than paying others not to produce, unless for genuine soil-conservation reasons. The small, family-farm operation should be encouraged through target-price mechanisms, which do not hurt the consumer, rather than through set-asides.

13. Productivity in industry should be approached on an industry-by-industry basis, carefully determining what can be done to encourage productivity growth.

14. The labor-management relations in Japan and West Germany need to be examined. We cannot — and should not — duplicate them in their entirety, but we should learn from them. West Germany, for example, gives labor a much greater voice in management decisions, with labor sitting on the board of most major corporations so that each side is in regular dialogue and understands the hopes and problems of the other. In Japan, corporations have an almost familial approach, which is markedly different from ours. Some American corporations have profitably studied these approaches and adopted portions of them successfully.

15. The Consumer Price Index should be corrected. There are massive flaws in the present index and an unbelievably cumbersome procedure in order to achieve change. It ought to be accurate. This correction in and of itself could be a major help in the inflation fight because sixty million Americans and many corporations have their income indexed in one way or another, almost always tied to the Consumer Price Index.

One of the more thoughtful economists on the Washington scene was the late Arthur Okun. He wrote:

> I find many analogies between accepting anti-inflation policies as a nation and going on a diet as an individual. Overeating is lots of fun and fundamentally enjoyable. Going on a diet is painful, and it brings few results in the short run. Procrastinating is never terribly serious; for the next bite will never kill you. And there is no clear-cut boundary line between normal weight and overweight. But the more we overindulge and the longer we procrastinate, the more serious the risk becomes. Once we get the message, we are tempted to go to the other extreme and adopt a starvation diet. The choices are never easy and they demand a great deal of maturity. We haven't yet demonstrated whether we have the maturity to adopt a sensible diet as a nation.[10]

CHAPTER FIVE

Jobs

Sometimes I hear people talking as if the great social advances have all been made, as if we have reached some type of high plateau that should simply be maintained. This is a myopic view of our society and of the world; it sees neither the great needs nor the tremendous potential of our nation. It urges us to guard our status quo while other nations advance. It is a posture insensitive to the substantial defects that remain in our national system. It overlooks the fact that the greatest division in our society today is not between blacks and whites, Hispanics and Anglos, haves and have-nots, but between those who have hope and those who do not.

There are many reasons for hopelessness. They relate to problems of race and language and economic status, although there is no perfect correlation with any of these.

In my years in political life I have talked with literally thousands who have felt "left out" by our society, who have seen no hope for themselves, who have viewed the future in only the bleakest terms, who have given up. The one characteristic most common in that group is the lack of a job. The American public is ready to accept the greatest stride forward this nation could make: to guarantee everyone a chance for a job.

For more than a century governments have recognized the job-creation function as important. Many nations are more successful at this task than we are. In 1848 the citizens of France heard these ringing words: "The provisional government of the French Republic undertakes to guarantee . . . work for every citizen."[1] And in our country Democrats and Republicans for decades have also noted the importance of creating jobs as a duty of government. In 1939 Senator

Ernest Lundeen of Minnesota said: "It is my belief that every man has the divine right to work. If he cannot find work in private industry, it is the duty of government to create work."[2] There are many things in the Soviet system of government I do not like, but one thing I applaud: guaranteed work for all their people. Can our free system of government do the same? Of course we can.

Poll after poll shows that the American public is willing to move to guarantee everyone the chance for a job. And poll after poll shows that the American people reject the only alternative: some type of guaranteed income, whether you work or not. Our society has backed into the less popular of the two, the guaranteed-income program, though we cloak it with a variety of other names. More than four decades ago we rejected the idea that if people cannot find work they should starve. Now we face the choice of either paying people for doing nothing or paying them for being productive. Our society has, for the most part, chosen the less sensible of those two choices.

Harry Hopkins, one of the nation's leaders during the 1930s, commented accurately: "Work relief costs more than direct relief but the cost is justified. First, in the saving of morale. Second, in the preservation of human skills and talents. Third, in the material enrichment which the unemployed add to our national wealth through their labors."[3]

Many protest that they do not understand the phenomenon of unemployment; they hear of all kinds of jobs available; the help-wanted sections of the newspapers are loaded with job possibilities. To those people I say: escape from your downtown office or pleasant suburbs and come with me to my district in which there is rural poverty, or visit much of urban America. What do you do if you are a fifty-five-year-old coal miner and the mine shuts down and all you know how to do is mine coal? What do you do if you live in an area of high unemployment and at forty-five your husband divorces you and you have no income and no skills? How do you get a job if you speak only Spanish and the employment forms they hand you are in English? Or if you are one of the millions of functionally illiterate Americans who cannot fill out a form, but you are ashamed to say you cannot read and write? How do you get a job if you have limited ability and you live in Alexander County, Illinois, where 27 percent of the population is on welfare or Pulaski County, Illinois, where 29 percent of the population is on welfare? How do you get a job in a manpower-glutted market when you are an ex-con? What if you were once on heroin and now have gone straight; who will hire you? What if you are an alcoholic who has overcome his or her problems but has a scarred employment record? Or worse yet, what if you are an alcoholic still struggling to overcome your problems? What if you are among the employable handicapped and part of the 50 percent of that group without a job? What if you are offered a job and discover that because of your handicap you can't get transportation to work? Or what if you are offered a job in another city and can't find housing that will structurally permit your wheelchair in the front door or in the bathroom?

The sweeping generalities also do not take into account people who for one reason or another are marginal in our society. George came to me desperate for a job, any job. He is perhaps forty years old, married, with three young children. One of his former employers told me that George is a good worker, but that he has a short temper and has a hard time getting along with his fellow employees. George recognizes his problem, though he blames everyone but himself. Our society's answer is to put him on welfare; we pay him to stay at home and do nothing but get angry with himself and the world — not good for him or for his wife and children.

Erma is single, perhaps thirty-five years old, with a slight speech defect. She is bright and friendly, but she is unable to sense a social situation properly (when and where to discuss toilet habits, for example) and she is an almost incessant talker. On two occasions I've been able to get jobs for her, but neither lasted long. She now is on welfare, eager to contribute something to society. She recognizes that our society has closed the door on her.

Leon is not mentally retarded, but close to it. His wife is about the same. He gets odd jobs occasionally from farmers, but they say he is unreliable in showing up for work and they call upon him only in an emergency. He is on welfare most of the time, but he manages even that poorly and frequently will go to a neighbor's back door to ask for milk or food scraps because his six children have nothing to eat.

These are all real cases. All three of these people share an eagerness to work, and yet they are now on welfare. Others among the unemployed include Ph.D.s or people otherwise highly specialized in their skills but suddenly in a society not demanding those particular skills. What do you do if you are an expert meatcutter, but suddenly at age fifty-eight you discover no one needs a meatcutter? Is the best answer for these people — and our society — simply to pay them for doing nothing? We can and must come up with better answers.

Our answers until the Reagan administration — primarily the Manpower Development and Training Act programs and the Comprehensive Employment and Training Act (CETA) — were viewed as temporary answers "until the private sector gets back on its feet and provides full employment." Although the private sector will continue to provide the bulk of employment opportunities, and should be encouraged to do more, the reality is that unemployment will be a permanent phenomenon in our society. Temporary, stopgap, Band-Aid programs will not solve the problem. The permanence of unemployment is due to the increasing flow of people, particularly women, into the labor market, the diminishing demand for people without special skills, and the increasing unmarketability of certain special skills (such as coal mining).

Since World War II we have never provided as much as 1 percent of our employment from public-service jobs. If we are to solve the difficulties confronting our nation, that low rate of public-service employment cannot continue. Certainly the Reagan administration's answer — cut back on jobs and build more prisons — is not the right answer. There were 9.5 million people unemployed at the end of 1981, and unless some significant new government program is begun that I do not foresee, that number will not fall below six million during the balance of this century. There are those who say that some among those listed as unemployed are people who should not be so listed. For example, one man had worked for a plant that closed; he has a promise of another job in six weeks; in the interim, he draws unemployment compensation and is listed among the unemployed. Whether or not his unemployment should technically be listed is not a matter of great national import; the important point is that he does not present a great dilemma to the nation. But more than a million fall into a category the Bureau of Labor Statistics calls "the discouraged worker," the person who has simply given up hope of finding a job and is no longer even trying. That one-million-plus group is not counted in the unemployment statistics because these people are not actively seeking work. My guess is that the 9.5 million figure of unemployed is close to accurate because those who do not get counted more than compensate for those counted who are not seeking employment.

If we have a substantial unemployment problem — and ours is greater than in most industrialized nations — and if the present answers are inadequate, what should we be doing? A sound employment program should include *at least* these points:

1. encouragement of job creation by the private sector;
2. an education program that trains young people for job opportunities and retrains adults whose skills have become outdated;
3. a project-oriented national jobs program that guarantees jobs at the minimum wage to almost all of those who cannot find jobs in the private sector.

The third part of this program is a significant departure from our present system, but it is not without precedent. Despite the Reagan attitude, Republicans as well as Democrats in the past have supported public-service jobs. President Richard Nixon, in a 1970 message to Congress, said: "Transitional and short-term public service employment can be a useful component of the nation's manpower policies."[4]

In his diary, the late Justice Felix Frankfurter said of someone: experience passes through him without leaving a mark.[5] I sometimes feel the same about our nation. We seem to need to learn and relearn the lessons of history, rarely noting that the wheel does not need to be reinvented. In the early 1930s we had an excellent jobs program in this country called the WPA (Works Progress Administration). Many of those who read this may have an image of people leaning on shovels, but in fact the WPA did precisely what we need to do today: turn a national liability (unemployed people) into an asset (productive people). Milton Katz has written: "It has been the central task of free men in this century to adjust the new demand to the old wisdom."[6] That is what we must do with unemployment.

A jobs experiment called the "Supported-Work Experiment" has taken place recently on a small scale. Four groups of people who are hard to place in jobs were selected — a total of ten thousand people. The categories were mothers on the Aid to Families with Dependent Children (AFDC) program, ex-drug addicts, former convicts, and inner-city youth. Less than one-fourth had completed high school; in the case of the youths, less than 1 percent. Fourteen percent of the AFDC mothers had never worked; 5 percent of the ex-addicts; 11 percent of the ex-offenders; and 22 percent of the inner-city youth. The AFDC mothers had been on welfare an average of 8.6 years. The ex-addicts had spent an average of two-and-a-half years in prison; the ex-offenders just under four years; and the youths an average of twenty-one weeks. These people were found in fifteen different localities and compared with a similar sample of those who did not have a jobs program. Costs per employee turned out to be a little higher than CETA public-service employment average costs.

The result for the AFDC mothers was striking. Double the number left the welfare rolls compared to the sample who had not been given jobs. The program had "its largest impact on the individuals with the least prior employment experience."[7] The permanent job impact on ex-addicts was much less dramatic, though it led to "a dramatic reduction in criminal activities."[8] The ex-addicts in this experiment had a 24-percent lower arrest rate compared to the controlled sample not given jobs, particularly reductions in robbery and drug-related offenses. For ex-offenders and youths (a requirement for eligibility was that at least 50 percent of the youths had to have delinquency records), the results are less clear — beneficial but much less dramatically so. In the case of the AFDC mothers and the ex-addicts, there are not only social benefits that accrue to children and families and neighborhoods, but clearly net savings above costs when studied over a period of twenty-seven months. For the youth group, costs exceeded direct economic benefits to the taxpayers by $2,400; for ex-offenders there was probably a greater cost than direct economic benefit, though further studies are underway to determine this. The longer-range benefits to these people and to society are overwhelmingly favorable, whether measured in economic or in social terms. (One interesting aspect for AFDC mothers is the decline in Medicaid costs. People who are working are healthier; among other things, they have less time to sit and reflect on what possible disease may be afflicting them.)

The groups in this test included particularly hard-to-place unemployed people with a special program designed to provide help in a transition to the world of work. Any successful jobs plan must include programs to concentrate extra help for those who labor under a special handicap, whatever its nature. Although the WPA program of the 1930s primarily helped the nonhandicapped, those with special problems were among its major beneficiaries.

What did the WPA do? Under that program, 651,000 miles of roads were built or improved, 125,110 buildings such as schools and libraries were erected or modernized, 16,100 miles of water line and 24,300 miles of sewerage facilities were put in. Hot lunches were served and day-care centers started, and 1.5 million illiterate adult Americans learned how to read and write. Histories were written, plays produced, and the culture of the nation immeasurably enriched.

Only one person per family was permitted to work on the WPA. Most who worked were unskilled, but some were not; up to 10 percent of those employed could be people not on the relief rolls. That figure stayed under 5 percent and generally encompassed the supervisors. Most on WPA were not permitted to work forty hours a week, so they could seek other employment in the remaining hours. If, because of sickness or job hunting, the hours allotted to them could not be worked, they could make them up in succeeding weeks. The program started through an executive order of Franklin D. Roosevelt in May 1935, and by December of that year 2,667,000 people were working. The WPA donated $6 per man per month to nonlabor costs of projects, so that local governments or states that did not have the money to buy tools and equipment could buy some of the basics.

A WPA-type project-oriented jobs program could be implemented again today. What advantages does that have over a CETA-type program? In many cases the CETA work could mesh with project orientation. In Illinois, for example, one enterprising township supervisor, Glenn Snider, persuaded the local Rotary Club to buy a car to drive senior citizens to stores, doctors' offices, and so on. Then he contacted the CETA prime sponsor to provide a driver. This is a township-oriented CETA public-service program. If CETA had a project orientation that included the goal of providing transportation to senior citizens, the result could be the same. CETA workers are generally more geared to institutions (cities, counties, nonprofit organizations, etc.) than to projects. The result is sometimes a less than effective utilization of personnel. In many places CETA workers simply replace the workers who would otherwise be employed, thereby becoming a subsidy for the city or entity involved, rather than a job-creation effort. The figures vary on how much substitution actually takes place; under the amendments to CETA passed in 1978, substitution has become substantially more difficult. In any event, it involves appreciably less than one-fifth of the total number of CETA workers.

I do not want to be misunderstood. I have been one of CETA's strongest supporters in Congress, for it has been almost the only visible alternative to welfare. CETA is unpopular, but the citizens and legislators and president who are demolishing the program without offering an alternative are simply asking for the growth of our welfare rolls, an even less popular program.

If a WPA-type proposal were revived, what projects would be possible? Here are a few of literally thousands of examples of what could be done:

• Plant 200 million trees a year; this would help clean our air, preserve our topsoil, ease our energy problem, and improve the appearance of the nation.

• Provide personnel for day-care centers so that mothers with small children who want to work can work. Some of these mothers could be personnel for day-care centers.

• Teach functionally illiterate people how to read and write. Many of those out of work who are highly literate could be helpful, working under the supervision of a trained teacher. We have somewhat more than ten million functionally illiterate people in this country, a substantial drag on the economy.

• Help teach Americans other languages. Many of those who are out of work are people whose mother tongue is not English. Some could serve as aides in schools or in adult-education programs.

• Develop hiking trails in national forests.

• Assist state and local governments in developing parks and playgrounds.

• Repair and build sidewalks.

• Help provide transportation for senior citizens and handicapped citizens where it is not available.

• Help keep subway and bus stations clean in large cities, in effect providing added security simply by being present.

• Assist in community-to-community mail delivery. Under the present postal arrangement, mail frequently goes hundreds (sometimes thousands) of miles when it could go ten or twenty miles directly between two communities. A few trips between communities could speed mail delivery and encourage more postal revenue because people would get better service.

• Provide rural areas far from health delivery services with visits from someone who could take blood-pressure counts, check for tooth decay, and provide a minimal type of health-information service, not to replace professionally trained medical personnel but to supplement them, particularly in rural areas where there is a severe shortage of trained medical and dental help.

• Construct bicycle paths along the highways of the nation where there is ample right-of-way, serving our health needs and our energy needs.

• Establish cultural-enrichment programs. In one area it might be an orchestra; in another, a project for an attractive mosaic for each public-housing project; in still another, an oral history program in which the local leaders are interviewed and their recollections recorded. The same can be done with older people in the community who may not have served in public office but can describe in great detail what it was like in past decades in that community.

• Insulate and improve the homes of the older poor in a community, working with the building trades in this project.

• Clean and enhance the attractiveness of old, neglected cemeteries in rural areas.

• Help maintain national, state, and city parks, which are sometimes poorly kept for lack of personnel. Significant improvement in the nation's recreation and relaxation opportunities could be achieved.

• Work with the railroads and the railroad unions to get badly neglected rail beds repaired, reducing accidents, improving rail service, and improving the financial health of the railroads.

• Tear down condemned buildings that are unsightly and havens for rats. Assess the cost to the property owner if he or she can be located.

The list can go on and on. With each of these project ideas there are some difficulties, but none are insurmountable. And some can be resolved by a good structure for the entire plan. My suggestion is that in all areas a local council should be appointed. In rural America the county is a natural jurisdiction line; in suburban and urban areas a smaller division of responsibility is probably desirable. The council would approve the projects and the appointment of the administrator of the program. It could be composed of twelve or thirteen people from labor, business, and a broad representation in the community. (Neither labor nor management is involved with the present manpower programs as much as they should be.) No project could proceed without the council's approval; in that way possible friction from labor unions, businesses, or other local groups can be avoided. It can be structured so that on the average one supervisor is employed for each ten unemployed people entering the project work force. Unions could see it as a means of employing more, not fewer, of their members. Assuming two million people would get jobs under such a program, a total of two hundred thousand supervisors would be needed, many of them union personnel. Business people would be on the council to make sure the project does not cause an uproar in the business community. If, for example, there is a national tree-planting program and the local nursery objects, the council would have the authority to decide not to utilize the tree project in their jurisdiction, even though it is moving ahead nationally.

The council and the local executive could initiate projects on their own, subject to the approval of a regional official and subject to budgetary limitations.

The program might be set up in this way for individuals: those employed under this proposal would have to be unemployed for at least thirty days. They would receive the minimum wage and work four days a week. At that rate, the income for a full year's work would be $5,574. Some would be eligible for additional welfare because of medical costs, size of family, and so on. No one from a family with a total income of $15,000 a year or more would be eligible. A husband and wife — both out of work more than thirty days — would be eligible for such a job program; together they would have a gross family income of more than $11,000. Four days a week is suggested because that permits one working day when the person could be seeking a job in the private sector that would pay more — even at the minimum wage, if it were a five-day-a-week job. The idea should be to provide public employment if private work is not available.

The final report on the WPA, written in 1946, includes this advice: "Federal, state and local governments, in order to meet changing conditions, would [be wise to] plan their public works well in advance . . . they should be prepared with plans to launch useful public works promptly to cushion large-scale unemployment. . ."[9]

That is still sound advice today. Here are the questions I hear most frequently when I mention this proposal, and my responses to them.

Would such a program be inflationary?

There are economists who will say that it is, that the only successful way to decrease inflation is to increase unemployment. Other economists take a differing view. My strong belief is that it would be *deflationary*. It is a belief based in part on history. Since World War II those periods with the least inflation have generally been periods of high employment. That follows common sense. It is inflationary to pay people for being nonproductive. Economic theories, such as the Phillips Curve, developed before we had protection mechanisms for the unemployed and desperate, have limited applicability to today's situation. In 1929, for example, fewer than 1 percent of the American work force was protected by unemployment compensation. Under this jobs proposal, the discouraged worker, now completely out of our productive system, would reenter it. And the teenager who does not have the opportunity to learn good work habits would have that opportunity, a substantial long-run investment for the nation. The person who has lost a sense of pride because he or she is not contributing to society could see a tree grow that he or she has planted, could see children helped in a day-care center, could have the opportunity to say, "I'm playing my part," and that seems to me no small gain in a participatory democracy. If we pay people for being productive, rather than for being nonproductive, everyone benefits.

These possible projects all add to the productive capacity of the nation and/or the enrichment of our national life. Repairing the railroad beds, for example, has been cited as a possible project. One train starts in my district at Saline County and goes three hundred miles north to Chicago hauling coal. On most of this route, trains go at a maximum of eight miles per hour under Commerce Commission ruling, because the railroad bed is bad. I pick up the *Wall Street Journal* and read about a shortage of coal cars. There is really not a shortage of coal cars. Rather, we have let our railroad beds deteriorate so that we are not efficiently utilizing coal cars. And all along the railroad track — because often the poor live near the railroad tracks — there are people who are drawing unemployment compensation or welfare who would like to be working. If we have the good sense to put two and two together, we will end up with happier, more productive people and a better rail system. And that is not inflationary.

Such a jobs program also is interconnected with the quality problem in the nation, for people without work habits could learn them, could learn to do something well. And parents who through fear or frustration do not leave their homes could get out, enlarging their horizons and the horizons of the young people in that home.

It should be of more than passing interest that the nations of Western Europe, which have substantially less inflation than we, generally spend more on manpower programs. These nations have achieved lower inflation rates without resorting to our levels of unemployment.

Doesn't our society need what the economists call "necessary frictional unemployment" (a small pool of unemployed people which is necessary to "lubricate" the economy of a nation)?

If such a program is enacted, there will not be total elimination of unemployment, but only the elimination of lengthy unemployment. Since about half of those who are unemployed are out of work thirty days or less, there still will be substantial numbers unemployed from that factor alone. In addition, there will be those who will be moving or, for one reason or another, will be unemployed longer than thirty days, depending in part on how unemployment-compensation and welfare programs would be restructured. We will still have more unemployment than many nations.

What would such a program cost?

No one knows with any certainty, but a reasonable estimate is that, if a full-blown program were to be suddenly thrust upon the nation, the cost at the most would be not more than $15 billion.[10] Fifteen billion dollars is about the amount by which Congress increased the defense appropriation in 1981 above what the Joint Chiefs of Staff and the president requested, about 35 percent of the 1982 increase.

In reality, however, no such program would descend in one fell swoop on the nation, though a great advantage of these programs is that we can move fairly swiftly to implement them. A respected researcher on the CETA public-service employment program has noted: "We were struck by the workability and speed of implementation of the public service employment program. . . . Many of the people involved in the monitoring study . . . had substantial doubts at the outset about the program and were surprised by the findings of the first two rounds of field research."[11] But any program would have to start gradually. Once a jobs program were enacted, priorities would have to be set, because there will be times and places where there are not enough jobs for all who want them. But suppose a program were started with veterans getting first preference, families with no one else in the program getting second preference, and areas of high unemployment targeted first. Perhaps a fixed number of rural counties and urban areas could be targeted the first year, both as a practical way to get the program going and as a way to test its strengths and weaknesses and improve on it.

Any such program would reduce costs appreciably for welfare and unemployment compensation. There is almost general agreement that these two programs need reexamination anyway. Present expenditures for other manpower programs also could be reduced.

Those in the jobs program should be required to pay Social Security, just as they would on any other job. This provides them added protection and at the same time provides additional sustenance to the Social Security trust fund, both in short-term needs and in the long-run picture.

But there is no question that such a jobs program would cost money. If the net cost were even $20 billion (a high figure), that would be less than 3 percent of the total national budget. The annual cost of the Reagan tax cut will be $150 billion. The job-creation costs are much less through direct public-service employment than through tax cuts (sometimes also needed) or public-works projects (also needed). And we should keep in mind Arthur Okun's law, that a 1-percent reduction in unemployment means an increase in the national income (GNP) of 3.2 percent. Some think that Okun's figure should now be lowered, but there is no question that as we lower unemployment, we enrich the nation economically as well as socially.

Economic common sense and the national need mesh. Ours is a society with a tradition of success through hard work; yet today many people do not feel they belong to such a society.

The party that has produced such pioneers in the employment field as Franklin Roosevelt, Senator Hubert Humphrey, and Representative Augustus Hawkins should also be the party that shows the nation the way to heal this festering, open economic sore.

"In the society of the future," the economist John Pierson wrote in 1944, "a job will rank with the right of free speech and other precious rights we consider fundamental to the preservation of human dignity.

The right to a job is more than getting an income; it is the right to perform a useful function and to preserve a respected social status. Psychologists, sociologists, and economists agree that long-continued unemployment distorts and destroys human personality."[12]

Who would support a full-employment program?

First, if a program is sound and necessary, we should start promoting it regardless of its immediate possibility of success. But in this case the support would be substantial. Polls show that the American public overwhelmingly supports such an idea. Labor unions would support it. Veterans groups probably would, if the veterans' preference plays a part in the decision. Business groups might well be persuaded to back it if they felt it could substantially reduce unemployment-compensation costs. The cities would support the program, for it would substantially relieve some of their fiscal problems. Even Republicans may not offer too much opposition when they recall that a proposal of Secretary of Labor George Schultz made in 1969 under the Nixon administration included a substantial public-service employment component. And the CETA legislation, passed by a Democratic Congress, was signed into law in 1973 by a Republican president.

There is one added benefit for Democrats if we sponsor such a program: we resume our rightful role as innovators. Pollster Peter Hart says that, while in the past the Democrats have been perceived as the creative force in government, the public now has shifted its perception to the Republicans as the innovators.[13]

The Democratic party did not achieve its pioneering role, its role as the champion of the nation's most fundamental needs, by pausing constantly and asking where the support would come for a program.

The need is there. The Republican party is unlikely to respond. The Democratic party must.

CHAPTER SIX

Industrial Modernization, Research, and Exports

"**W**hy is the American industrial giant starting to limp?" asks the U.S. Chamber of Commerce magazine *Nation's Business*. They answer their own question: "There is blame enough to go around. Business, the unions, government — all have contributed."[1] Even consumers have contributed, for as they have sought quality goods they have often turned to products made in Germany or Japan or Sweden or some other nation, whether for an automobile, coal-mining equipment, or a television set.

Democrats have stressed the "demand" side of the ledger in economic policy, and the Republicans have stressed the "supply" side. Both Republicans and Democrats can point to variations from that rule, but, on the whole, that has been the situation — as accurate as sweeping generalizations can be.

The Democratic party has said that, if you provide the average American with the means to purchase, then General Motors will sell cars and Sears will sell refrigerators. And that keeps employment up, and the happy economic circle keeps rolling. In addition, Democrats stress the demand side of things because they believe that this helps to solve the distribution problem in our society, giving every American the opportunity for a decent life.

Republicans have traditionally stressed a "trickle-down" economic theory: if you provide enough benefits and incentives to General Motors, then everyone in the society benefits. "We must develop the productive capacity of the nation and then our problems will be solved," they assure us. There has been no stronger champion of that view than Ronald Reagan. His budget imposed severe cuts on programs for the poor but included substantial benefits for the wealthy. On the "Issues and Answers" television program, Secretary of Health and Human Services Richard Schweiker responded to a question about a cutback for the poor with the comment that everyone has to sacrifice in order to stop inflation. Reporter James Wooten asked him what sacrifice someone in his income category had to make and he provided a less-than-satisfactory answer. Wooten repeated the question and, when pressed, Schweiker said his children would have to join others in paying more for school lunches. The nature of the Reagan program is such that someone in the upper-income brackets has to search for a sacrifice the budget cuts will impose. The poor are cut on almost every program that benefits them. For example, although aid to handicapped children and school-lunch programs is decreased, high-bracket income-tax rates are reduced from 70 to 50 percent.

A balance is needed. If General Motors has the ability to produce but there is no demand, no one gains. On the other hand, if demand is present but productive capacity is not, we are at an equally disastrous impasse.

That fundamental economic debate will continue, but its relevance to our current situation is limited. After the 1980 election, and after four years as the most respected member of the Carter White House staff, Stuart Eizenstat gave his party this advice: "We must shift our emphasis . . . to policies which encourage greater investment in productivity."[2]

Almost imperceptibly the world's economic picture has changed. Yesterday's slogans and policies do not necessarily fit today's realities. The debate of the past decades has been within a nation that dominated the world economically (and in almost every other way) and assumed that such a condition would continue indefinitely. Mixed in with that assumption was a touch of arrogance. A wealthy friend told me a few years before his death: "God gives in abundance to those who are good." Since my friend had in abundance, the assumption had to be that he was somehow a little more virtuous than most people. And there has been a touch of this in our national attitude.

But while we basked in our smugness, Japan and West Germany, as the most dramatic examples, emerged with our help from the disaster of war recognizing that industrial change and modernization are necessary and continuing. The United States, a sleeping giant, is slowly awakening to a world that is appreciably different than we have known. We find many countries with higher per-capita income, greater productivity increases, and less inflation. Japan now takes an average of twelve hours to make a car, the United States thirty hours. The 1981 World Bank statistical report shows the United States now eighth worldwide in income per person. Ahead of us are Kuwait, Switzerland, Sweden, Denmark, West Germany, Norway, and Belgium. Only slightly behind us are the Netherlands and France. Until recently we viewed some of these countries as backward. Former Senator Frank Church has commented: "If we are seeing the end of 'the American era' it is not because we have lost the superpower race with the Soviet Union for strategic superiority, but because we are losing our capacity to compete with our own allies."[3]

From 1948 to 1972 U.S. agriculture reduced its demand for labor by 500 million man-hours per year, permitting sharp increases in productivity in other sectors of the economy through the released manpower.[4] Since 1972 we have had a much stabler labor situation in agriculture, and that is being felt in nonagricultural productivity. Weapons production is also consuming great quantities of labor, research, and highly technical skills, hindering somewhat our research and productive capacities in other areas (a hindrance other industrial nations experience also, but to a lesser degree).

The picture is not all bleak. We are still by far the most economically significant nation on the earth. And the American industrial worker generally still produces more per hour than his or her counterpart in any other nation, though that gap is narrowing.

In many sectors the quality gap has not only closed, but our friends in other countries have surpassed us. A renewed emphasis on quality production has to be much more a part of the nation's economy, and it can be. Honda motorcycles are manufactured in Marysville, Ohio, as well as in Japan, but with one difference. As William Bumgarner, the paint-room supervisor in the Ohio plant, has noted: "Ours are much better."[5] And apparently that is an accurate assessment. The *Wall Street Journal* notes that the Ohio Honda plant "drums into its employees the credo that quality products and job security are linked." A twenty-four-year-old employee, Rick Wilgus, says: "As long as we put in good quality, people will keep buying our products, in which case I'm going to have a job." As in Japan, the Ohio plant goes out of its way to play down distinctions between employees and management, with no separate parking spaces for executives, everyone eating in the same cafeteria, and identical Honda uniforms for all. The combination of these and other policies results in high production figures and high quality.

There are three bright fields where we are ahead of every other nation: agriculture, aerospace, and computers. All three have risen to their present position because of private sector–public sector cooperation. Agriculture would not be the backbone of our export market were it not for agriculture-extension and education programs and soil-conservation activities. The same private-public effort is there in the aerospace and computers areas, as well.

Second, all three have benefited from a great amount of research. When, with government support, universities and seed companies produced better corn and soybeans, they did not stop there but continued research. The jet engines of yesterday were remarkable, but cannot compare to today's more improved product. The computers of twenty years ago worked wonders, but are primitive compared to today's. In all three areas, no one is saying: "We're ahead of everyone. Let's rest on our laurels."

Third, all three sectors are extremely conscious of the importance of exports to their industry. Twenty years ago farmers were vaguely aware that exports were important to American agriculture; today they are remarkably aware of it, as two presidents who have imposed embargoes have discovered. If it were not for the export sales of our aerospace technology, computers, and agriculture — the three totaled $37,554 million in exports the first half of 1981 — our balance of trade and our domestic economic situation would be much worse. The overall United States record in exports is spotty; in four of the last five years they did not balance with imports. Oil is the obvious cause for this imbalance, but that is too easy an explanation. The large majority of American corporations that should be exporting are not. In the last decade the United States lost 23 percent of its share of the world industrial export market — some of that to be expected — a loss of more than two million jobs. Each $1 billion in exports results in forty thousand jobs.

U.S. Exports	Dollars (millions)
Computers	$ 2,957
Aerospace	8,686
Agriculture	25,911

Those three qualities — research, cooperation between government and the private sector, and export consciousness — loom much larger in countries such as West Germany and Japan, our competitors in the non-Communist world, and they are present where the United States has been successful.

The AFL-CIO has suggested that a national reindustrialization board consisting of members of the public, labor, and industry should be created. Much more important, they suggest a series of similar miniboards on a sector-by-sector basis. The idea is excellent. It guarantees no cures for our ills; but there is at least a reasonable possibility that if, twenty years ago, a group of representatives from the steel industry, the steel union, and the public (including government) had been meeting regularly, asking searching questions of themselves and others, the steel industry in the United States would not be as outmoded as it now finds itself. The coal industry has great domestic-market potential, the possibility of a stunning growth in exports, but discouraging productivity statistics. What can be done to encourage greater productivity? How do we encourage more research — and greater utilization of existing research — on the high-sulfur coal problem? How do we encourage expansion of port facilities so that we can meet export demand? A reindustrialization board could probe these and other questions. It could guide both the public and private sectors in healthier directions. It could encourage the public-private cooperation so familiar to Japan, West Germany, and Korea. The bottlenecks of regulation and other problems can be tackled together much more effectively.

You can't sell if you're not even trying. Eighty percent of the American businesses that should be exporting are not. Part of the reason they are not is lack of the federal government's encouragement. We are the only major industrial nation with no separate government department for export sales. If the climate is not ripe to create that, there clearly needs to be *at a minimum* a much greater emphasis on exports by the present Department of Commerce. Commercial attachés stationed with U.S. embassies abroad should be better grounded in the nuts and bolts of American business, and there are some signs of improvement. Our tax policies should not discourage U.S. business exports. Business schools should have a much greater international emphasis; even most Ph.D.s in business have had no international business courses. And all schools must awaken to the fact that we are literally behind every other nation on the face of the earth in language study. We are the only country in which you can go through elementary school, high school, college, and graduate school and never have a year of a foreign language. You can't sell your products effectively if you can't speak the language of the customer. The day we could demand that our customers talk to us in English is past; but our school system has not recognized that reality.*

We need a thoughtful, solid program to stimulate more research. The quality of American products must constantly improve. To get there we need added tax incentives for corporations to increase their research efforts. This should be kept relatively simple. For example, for every $1.00 a corporation spends for research, it could deduct as an expense $1.20 instead of $1.00. The benefits of probing for new ideas through tax preference go beyond the obvious. Not only would it stimulate research, but it could shift the emphasis of many corporations from acquisitions and mergers as means of achieving growth to research and better products. As *Newsweek* noted: "Businessmen are growing increasingly unwilling to commit themselves to long-term expansion or basic research, concentrating instead on low-risk projects that produce quick returns."[6] The key word here is *basic,* for while our overall research efforts have experienced modest growth, basic research has been on a thirteen-year decline. Our research efforts also are more tilted toward the military than any country other than the USSR. While we are perfecting better missiles, others are working on better refrigerators and television sets and manufactured products that can be exported. Not long ago the textile industry appeared to be on its deathbed, but

---

*For a much more detailed look at our foreign-language deficiencies, see my book, *The Tongue-Tied American: Confronting the Foreign Language Crisis* (New York: Continuum Books, 1980).

modest research brought innovations and increased productivity, and although the textile industry still has serious problems, it is alive and far from death. The news is not all good, however. Most of the research took place in other countries, so that the new and better machines are being imported from Switzerland, Japan, Italy, and West Germany. But now American textiles are being exported.

We also need much more encouragement — instead of the present discouragement — of the creative minds of this nation, the inventors who in their homes putter and tinker and come up with amazing ideas. I have worked with a variety of patent holders in my district and I have yet to find one who has received any help from the U.S. government. I could cite instances of discouragement, however. It does not surprise me that the U.S. Patent Office now issues more patents to citizens of Japan, West Germany, and the Soviet Union than to United States citizens. It takes more than twenty-two months to get a patent approved, and according to *U.S. News and World Report,* pirating of inventions has become a fairly common practice. The article quotes a president of a technology company: "Stealing inventions has become an accepted business practice for big companies since they know they can probably beat the system. The little guy hardly has a chance."[7] The article concludes that "reforms in the patent process could fire the kind of American genius that produced so many innovations in the past." Good ideas are not stimulated, and that must change.

And just as through the years we have had a conscious policy of encouraging agricultural research at our state universities, or medical research at those same schools and at the National Institute of Health, so we must in some conscious manner determine some federal priorities for research and put more of our federal tax dollars in those directions.

In all of these decisions, there is a delicate line to be walked: How far should government be involved? Some, like the Republican governor of Wisconsin, say, "We need the federal government to defend the nation, deliver the mail, and get the hell out of our lives."[8] My guess is that the governor feels differently about federal milk programs or other areas that directly affect his state. The marketplace generally should determine the course of the nation's productive direction. But blindly following that lead is as foolhardy as those who would take the opposite extreme and have government the dominant force in all decision making.

What more can and should the government do?

We need to create an agency similar to the former Reconstruction Finance Corporation. That agency — through its loan-making power — could help to make decisions on which industries need special encouragement and could help to plan for a transition for industries that will be eliminated by some new domestic or foreign development. Cases such as those of Lockheed and Chrysler would be referred to this agency. Their number, unfortunately, is likely to grow. Congress's awkward decision making depends more on pressure and sentiment than on facts. The agency and its chief executive office should be so constructed as to minimize political pressures. But more important than dealing with yesterday's and today's failures, or near failures, such a board should be probing where the United States ought to be twenty years from now. Japan is doing this. West Germany is doing this. We are not. This ought to be a joint business-government agency to attract to its board some of the most incisive minds in both of these fields. We need to plan for success, not simply to rescue semifailures.

Representative Morris Udall of Arizona suggests that we take a hard look at the corporate structure of the nation. Both business and the public could benefit by such a study. Twenty years ago four hundred of the nation's corporations controlled two-thirds of the corporate wealth of the nation. Today two hundred corporations do; under the Reagan administration the figure will get worse. Does the public benefit when DuPont takes over Conoco, taking money that might go into research and using it for acquisition? We must make certain that the free-enterprise system is really free, that competitive forces are at work. "Consumer sovereignty" becomes almost a hollow term when the consumer does not have meaningful choices. And to the extent competition diminishes and choices disappear, the nation is likely to see increased consumer political activity, as well as inflationary pressures. However, some accommodations should be made for American corporations that must compete in the world market with businesses that do not operate under such restraints as the Sherman Anti-Trust Laws. Exemptions might also be made from the antitrust laws for cooperative research on specific problems that confront an industry.

I confess some preference for programs that encourage capital formation without economic concentration. West Germany, for example, has a policy of matching $1 for each $7 an individual invests in common stocks, if the family income is below a certain level. That helps income distribution as well as capital formation. Representative Richard Schulze, a Republican from Pennsylvania, has suggested that 10 percent of capital investment be tax deductible, up to a maximum of $1,000 on a $10,000 investment. That would encourage both capital formation and the small investor. When the issuance of stock becomes less attractive, borrowing becomes more likely. Here also there are difficulties, in addition to excessively high interest rates, for the less than 5-percent savings rate in the United States is significantly lower than the rate of other nations — less than half as much as our Canadian neighbors; one-third as high as Great Britain, France, and West Germany; and one-fourth as much as Japan and Italy. Part of the difficulty — how much is a matter of dispute — is our tax structure. Japan, for example, exempts interest from savings accounts up to $50,000. Germany has a system that encourages multiyear saving, an idea I like because it permits banks and savings-and-loans institutions to make long-term commitments with greater certainty. Further protection for those who save is desirable; it will provide additional capital for housing and industrial development and will have some impact on interest rates, reducing them slightly. In our country we discourage saving by permitting consumer-indebtedness interest to be deducted at income-tax time. Interest payments on housing or a car should be deductible, but should the same go for interest payments to the local department store or American Express? The United States is almost alone among nations in permitting that deduction.

We are overregulated. I mention this with some hesitancy, for there are too many barn burners who want to do away with fundamental safeguards our society needs. The nation has to have safety regulations on air flights and on mining, for example. But we have become overregulated, though progress in reducing regulations has been made. Jimmy Carter reduced air, truck, and railroad regulations dramatically and significantly lessened the regulation morass in agencies such as the Occupational Safety and Health Administration (OSHA). But every study I have seen shows that one of the reasons for our lack of productivity growth is excessive regulation. It is not regulation designed by people with ill intent that causes the problem, but occasionally we have a sensible mandate taken to extremes by sincere people. Let me give you an illustration. In some schools young women were not being admitted to agriculture classes and young men could not get into home-economics classes. There were some huge disparities in the use of federal funding in physical education. So Congress passed legislation saying there should be no discrimination on the basis of sex. When the regulations came out, they prohibited schools from having father-son banquets or mother-daughter banquets, something no one in Congress even considered. The federal government does not need to decide such a matter. But it should decide whether federal funding for high school agriculture classes requires that girls should be admitted to such classes.

Speed, stability, and coordination are also regulatory problems.

If regulations require approval of a government agency, that agency ought to be required to respond promptly. Regulatory delay is a costly reality to the U.S. business community. A critic of these delays, economist Lester Thurow, commented: "Give me $200,000 and I'll stop any project for five years."[9] We should be more careful in initially adopting regulations, but slow to change them once adopted. Industries are tired of the unpredictability of regulations under which they operate. One economist comments: "The uncertainty about what will come out of Washington has been the biggest negative on productivity. Today nobody in his right mind would build a new steel mill, for example, because he wouldn't know if it could meet whatever the regulations are when it's completed."[10] Greater coordination is also needed. One agency says one thing, another the opposite. A federal agency may give strikingly different instructions from those given by a state agency. Some use the phrase "regulatory jungle" and sometimes that is not an inaccurate description.

We must build a better labor-management climate. Too many coal miners don't feel the coal companies care about them; too many auto workers feel the car manufacturers couldn't care less about them; and management too often feels that labor is irresponsible. I do not suggest that we can create the type of familial industrial situation Japan has; nor should we mandate the labor voice in management policy West Germany has; but we can learn from these countries. We have grown accustomed to hostility rather than cooperation in too many industries; both sides live comfortably with this adversarial relationship because they know where they stand. (I might add that we also seem to enjoy the government-versus-business adversarial relationship, which also is unprofitable and shortsighted.) But would it do any harm for more corporations to have a union president or representative on their boards, after the model of Chrysler, which elected United Auto Workers president Douglas Fraser? (And it would do no harm for corporations with significant environmental concerns to have that input on a corporate board.) There have been some startling increases in productivity, drops in absenteeism, and improvements in quality control where management and labor have worked together. Yet we are unwilling to profit from such examples of success. Why do we have seventeen times as many grievances per hundred thousand workers as West Germany? German corporations originally fought the idea of having union representation on their boards, but now they believe in it. Can we learn from this? The "quality-circle" idea, which brings a small group of management and labor people together regularly, went from its limited use in the United States, to extensive use in Japan, and now some of our people are coming back from Japan with this "new idea" they have discovered there. I do not suggest that the federal government can, by statute, create cooperation and stimulate improved product quality, but the president can lead in a direction of cooperation between management and labor by using what Theodore Roosevelt used to call the "bully pulpit" of the presidency.

Our industries must not only be export conscious, but also particularly sensitive to the developing nations. Ninety percent of the population growth from today until the end of the century will come in the developing nations. That does not mean that they will have that same proportion of economic growth, but that they will be the fastest growing factor in the world economic picture. Our research, production, and sales must shift dramatically to the new market realities.

We can combine employment needs with modest assistance to the business community. The New Jobs Tax Credit enacted in 1977 is not widely used, but those firms that have used it are pleased with the results. Another option is to give anyone out of work longer than a certain period (perhaps thirty days) a job ticket. With that ticket he or she could approach an employer; if hired, during the first eight weeks the job seeker works for the employer, the employer would receive $1 per hour as a direct grant from the federal government. That figure then would gradually decline in succeeding weeks to zero. The program has three advantages: it employs those who are unemployed, it has a slight antiinflation factor, and it can help the business.

We need to encourage long-range planning in business. How can a government that does so little long-range planning encourage business to do it? If the preacher sets an example along with delivering sermons, he is more likely to be listened to. The temptations in both government and business are similar. Policy makers and top administrators are anxious for quick results for their stockholders/voters. And sometimes the businessman/political leader who provides those quick results is doing it at the sacrifice of long-range gain. In commenting on the export-sales success of Boeing, General Electric, and Caterpillar, a *New York Times* article noted: "The export winners have typically taken a long-term approach to selling overseas; they are willing to wait years for the payoff, rather than becoming discouraged when, as is often the case, early years of spade work in markets produce few results. . . . Boeing . . . had a salesman in North Africa for seven years before he sold a single plane."[11] Japan has somehow built into her industrial structure an ability to look at the long-range picture that we have too seldom developed. If our governmental leaders simply urged the business leaders of this nation to take more of a long-range look at things, that simple sermon — however tarnished the preacher — would have some wholesome effect.

And unless that long-range look takes place, improvements in accelerated depreciation taxes or other tax changes will not do much. The average open-hearth furnace in a steel plant in the United States, for example, is thirty-three years old, not because of bad tax laws or environmental regulations, but because of shortsightedness. We cannot afford shortsightedness in business or in labor or in government.

CHAPTER SEVEN

Health Services

A program of complete health coverage by the government, similar to those in Great Britain, Canada, and many other nations, is not likely to pass Congress during the next decade. The major political parties in Great Britain and Canada support their medical programs and find them generally popular. But the mood in the U.S. Congress, in both political parties, is appreciably different.

Does that mean that we cannot move to meet the most pressing health needs of our society? I think not. The country is ready for some steps forward in health care. Except for dramatic situations that evoke dramatic responses, most legislative progress in the United States has been step by step, rather than by giant leaps.

Though many other nations make significant contributions to the state of health-care knowledge, the United States is first among nations in health research, a situation that is likely to continue. Our research can be faulted for responding to well-publicized needs rather than the less-visible but equally pressing health problems; but even with that valid criticism of research, the United States has made and is making remarkable strides and is far ahead of other countries. But in health delivery we are not number one by any statistical gauge. In health delivery the quality performance this nation must seek is too often lacking. A universally accepted statistic, for example, is the number of infant deaths per one thousand births. The United States ranks fourteenth on that list behind Sweden, Denmark, Japan, Finland, Norway, the Netherlands, France, Belgium, Canada, Singapore, Scotland, England and Wales, and the German Democratic Republic.

"In health there is freedom," nineteenth-century writer H. F. Amiel noted. "Health is the first of all liberties."[1] That liberty must be spread more widely.

What are our areas of greatest need?

1. Preventive health care.
2. Health care for pregnant women and young children.
3. Health care for senior citizens.
4. Health care for those with overwhelming medical expenses.

That list omits one obvious area: the ordinary citizen who is neither old nor pregnant, who does not have overwhelming medical bills, but who finds adequate health care too costly.

Preventive Health Care

Progress is being made, but preventive health care needs continued emphasis. In 1980 there were four times as many people in the United States who were eighty years old than there were in 1970 — in part an expected growth, but in part the result of programs such as food stamps. "An apple a day keeps the doctor away" is an old American saying that recognizes the value of preventive health care through nutrition. A German proverb says the same: "Better pay the butcher than the doctor." The food stamp program, although badly maligned by the public, has been responsible for almost unbelievable strides toward eliminating severe malnutrition in the United States. It is one of the most dramatically successful programs in the history of our country, yet it has little public support. I always hear about the woman in the grocery store who spends all her food stamps for steak and Pepsi-Cola. Such examples are real, but they are far from typical. They are real (though exaggerated) because often those who receive food stamps are not good managers; that is why many of them must resort to food stamps. Studies by the Field Foundation make clear that the food-stamp program has wrought remarkable changes in the health of Americans. There are still people in this country who are seriously malnourished, but only a fraction of those of the pre-food-stamp days. That means better health for these people. Those who suffer from malnutrition are much more susceptible to disease and have greater difficulty recovering. There was some legal abuse of the food-stamp program, but Congress acted to remedy this situation in 1979 and 1980. Yet when the Reagan administration came in, it asked for substantial cuts in the food-stamp program despite the fact that 93 percent of those on the program have incomes below the poverty line and 94 percent have less than $500 in liquid assets, including insurance policies.

Cleaner air and water have not only helped fish and trees, but human beings as well. Finding the practical answer to air and water pollution is not always easy. But it is not contradictory to be for clean air and more coal consumption, to favor industrial development and clean water. Every decision made by the federal and state environmental-control agencies has not been right, but the right answer cannot be to turn back the clock. We do not need to relax automobile pollution standards, as the Reagan administration has requested, for example. The *Chicago Tribune,* not a Democratic journal, noted that the Environmental Protection Agency director "seems to have been recruited for her job largely on the basis of the stridency of her opposition to toxic waste control legislation as a member of the Colorado legislature. . . . Mr. Reagan's style has been winning, and many of the things he's trying to do . . . deserve support. But as far as the environment is concerned, Mr. Reagan is a menace."[2]

The anticigarette campaign (which is not approved of by some of my colleagues representing tobacco states) has changed the nation's habits and has reduced the incidence of lung cancer. Efforts to encourage people to have their blood pressure checked are meeting with some success. Exercise, particularly running, is enjoying greater and greater popularity. Weight problems are now universally recognized as more than an aesthetic consideration; millions of Americans periodically resolve to lose a few pounds and sometimes do.

But more needs to be done and can be done without great expense. This includes the prevention programs already mentioned, plus:

• Regular physical checkups for everyone, at least at the most minimal level (blood pressure, heartbeat, teeth, etc.). It generally should not be a government program, but for people who cannot afford a checkup, one should be provided.

• Expansion of nutrition programs in schools and community centers.

• Accident- and fire-prevention programs. Smoke detectors should be placed in all public-housing units and public buildings, and their use should be encouraged in private homes and buildings.

• Expansion of intensive drug and alcohol education programs.

Health Care for Pregnant Women and Young Children

By guaranteeing expectant mothers and young children adequate health care, we will save literally billions of dollars in future years on medical expenditures and billions more in days that are not missed from school and work; we will influence our economy in a variety of positive ways. Congress has enacted a program authorizing such care for many pregnant women, and for children through the age of six. It has yet to receive the funding necessary to fully implement the program, but studies already show substantial long-run economic savings to the country.

Health Care for Senior Citizens

There are many who believe that the nation has taken care of our senior citizens through Medicare. But this 12 percent of the population pays more than 30 percent of the medical, hospital, dental, and pharmaceutical bills. Some programs, such as home visits, which often make nursing-home stays unnecessary, simply need to be expanded. In addition, a program of health care for the older portion of our population needs these major modifications:

Dentures, hearing aids, and eyeglasses should be included under Medicare. When I travel through my district one of the things I hear frequently is: "Paul, please excuse my appearance, but I can't afford false teeth." With all of the things we do, if we can't at least provide dentures for the people who have built our society, something is wrong. Hearing aids and eyeglasses also are necessities for many older people.

Hospital entrance fees should be modified. We charge a Medicare patient $260 when he or she goes into a hospital. By 1984 it will be $332. After paying that, Medicare in theory picks up the bills for these senior citizens. I say "in theory" because Medicare has certain allowable fees, and often older citizens covered by Medicare find themselves faced with substantial costs above the allowable fees. To add $332, which they must pay on entering a hospital, is an oppressive burden for many, astronomical for some, sometimes stopping people who should go to a hospital, sometimes reducing personal expenditures for food to almost nothing. And what about the person who goes into the hospital and eight months later has to go in again? The fee to be paid by the Social Security participant should be $25 or $50, to discourage unnecessary hospital entrance, but the present escalating charges should be changed. Other policies that need modification are payment for a private-duty nurse and the sixty- to ninety-day limitation on hospital and nursing-home stay.

The cost of out-of-hospital drugs should be partially covered by Medicare. When someone under Medicare goes into the hospital, drugs ordinarily are covered. But the same older citizen, upon checking out of a hospital, may find a monthly expenditure of $65 or more for filling prescriptions. It would be too costly for Medicare to assume the entire burden for these drugs. In addition, the experience in other countries suggests that some fee encourages careful utilization of drugs, rather than excessive use and waste. If we enacted a program under which the government paid for half the cost of out-of-hospital drugs, that would be of substantial help to the older population.

These changes would require some modification of the tax laws by the House Ways and Means Committee and the Senate Finance Committee to ensure the adequate funding of the Medicare Trust Fund, from which these changes would be financed. But the total costs are small, as government programs go, and the help to senior citizens would be significant.

Health Care for Those with Overwhelming Medical Expenses

A persistent problem that receives periodic attention in the media is that of the family that has a child with renal disease, or cancer, or some other problem and suddenly finds itself faced with overwhelming bills. Recently I had lunch with a small businessman. He has been a contractor and consultant, largely operating on his own, never employing many people. He did not incorporate. About two years ago he learned his wife had leukemia, and about eight weeks ago he had a serious heart attack that required a lengthy hospital stay. His medical bills have averaged $357 a day since his heart attack. He does not have insurance coverage. "Fortunately, my wife and I had a little nest egg, and our house is paid for. When our savings run out, we plan to sell the house. But the only thing that will save us from financial ruin is either a sudden improvement in our health status or death."

On another occasion a man told me that if he took the advice of physicians on an incurable disease he might live a year or two longer, but his family would lose everything. "I've decided to die and protect the family," he told me. And he did.

A couple came to me in a rural community recently. The man is sixty years old. A few months after leaving a government job with no Social Security coverage he had a serious heart attack. He has no health insurance. He had been in his new job with a grocery store only a few months, not long enough to establish Social Security coverage. His doctors advised him that he must have a major heart bypass operation if he is to have any hope of surviving. It will cost about $30,000. He and his wife have paid for their small home and he does not want to mortgage or sell it to pay for an operation he may not survive. "I'll just hope I can make it to sixty-two and get Medicare coverage," he told me, while his distraught wife said that the doctors don't think he can live that long without an operation. I am trying to work something out for him through a friend who is a physician. But as of the time I write this, I am uncertain what can be done.

The stories go on and on. They are real. They are tragic.

If we had a program under which a family that used more than 20 percent of its annual income on all forms of medical coverage would be reimbursed 90 percent of the balance over 20 percent, we would have a program that the federal government could afford and one that would provide great protection for all Americans. Here is a practical example of how it would work. A house painter whose family's income last year was $14,000 suddenly learns that his thirteen-year-old daughter has serious health problems, which result in a $53,000 hospital and medical bill. Twenty percent of a $14,000 income is $2,800.

$$\begin{array}{r} \$53,000 \\ -\quad 2,800 \\ \hline \$50,200 \\ \times \quad 90\% \\ \hline \$46,800 \end{array}$$

The federal government would assume $46,800 of the expenses. The family still would have a bill of $6,200 — no small amount — but they could work out arrangements with the doctors and the hospital to pay that back over a period of years. They could survive that. But $53,000 is impossible for them. By paying only 90 percent of the balance the government would be providing at least a mild restraint on escalating hospital and medical bills. The patient would have an interest in keeping costs down. But families and individuals could face something other than financial disaster on top of the physical and emotional strain of massive medical problems.

The first two points mentioned on page 56 — preventive health care and coverage for the pregnant and very young — have been accomplished to some extent. The last two programs can be effected for about one-sixth of the cost of a full national-health-insurance-coverage program. That still is a great deal of money — about $22 billion — but it could be enacted step by step over several years as government income grows, or it could be covered by a slight tax increase. It should be noted that $22 billion is about half the increase President Reagan asked for defense programs in one year, or one-seventh of the recent tax cut.

A health program that meets our most pressing needs is not beyond the realm of possibility, even in these times of fiscal austerity.

CHAPTER EIGHT

Education

S omeone asked Aristotle how much educated people are superior to the uneducated and he replied: "As much as the living are to the dead."[1] That is obviously an exaggeration of no small proportions, but it is true that an education offers personal cultural-enrichment opportunities. Surveys consistently show that college graduates find more satisfaction and happiness in life than those without college experience. On the average, the person with the greater education will earn more than the person with the lesser education. Adam Smith noted that in 1776. The nation that stresses education will generally achieve more economic progress than the nation that does not, although it is intriguing that there is a major new book, *Revitalizing America*, written by an educator, hardly mentioning education as part of the process of revitalizing the nation.[2] The education community has some public relations to do! But the needs are significantly greater than simply an improved image.

Ezra Vogel, in his book *Japan As Number One*, points out that in the United States the average elementary and high-school student attends school 180 days a year, and the Japanese counterpart attends an average of 250 days a year. Soviet students go to school six days a week rather than five. A Soviet high-school (secondary-school) graduate has had at least one foreign language each year since either the first or fourth grade, has had five years of physics, four of chemistry, five of geography, and five of biology. By comparison, 9 percent of U.S. high-school graduates have had one year of physics and 16 percent have had one year of chemistry; we are also woefully behind the Soviets in foreign-language study.

The Japanese and Soviet illustrations suggest that "coasting" educationally is hardly in the national interest. But our problems are larger and more complex than simply the competition from other nations. Although the United States spends $200 billion per year on education — 8 percent of our GNP — our nation has some obvious needs and problems, including:

• Greater attention must be paid to the schools in urban and rural areas where poverty is concentrated. Quality is far from what it should be.

• For eighteen consecutive years — until 1981 — there has been a steady drop in the Scholastic Aptitude Test (SAT) scores of U.S. high-school seniors. And the percentage of those taking the test who score in the upper 20 percent of possible scores has dropped steadily. Schools from the elementary level through college too often have becomes places of comfort rather than learning.

• Somewhere between ten and twenty million adult Americans are functionally illiterate, a problem that has been virtually ignored.

• More assistance is needed for school programs for the handicapped. The federal government properly mandated that these young people should be helped. But the level of federal assistance is far less than it should be.

• The United States lags behind every other nation in foreign-language training. This harms our trade and security, as well as our culture.

• Colleges and universities (particularly the private schools) will undergo some severe financial problems during the coming decade and many fine schools probably will have to fold.

• At the elementary and secondary level, many private schools also face serious fiscal difficulties.

• Those who plan to be teachers are declining in ability-measurement scores, and many of the finest teachers are leaving the profession.

• Vocational education needs reevaluation and support.

• Educational opportunities for the adult citizen must become a much greater part of the scene than they are at present.

• We are among the few nations that charge students for higher education. In most countries higher education is free, and comes with a small monthly living allowance, similar to the program made available to veterans immediately after World War II. Even with all that is offered needy students, many still find they cannot afford to go to college, and probably still more simply find themselves confused by the multiplicity of programs and agencies. Tens of thousands cannot attend college for financial reasons.

• There is, finally, an overall need for greater stress on quality in American education. A friend commented recently: "The one thing I like about high-school and college sports is that this is the only area in the entire field of education where quality is recognized and rewarded." That is an exaggeration, but it contains some truth. The nation needs a resurgence of an aim toward quality in general, and education is no exception to that need.

Higher Education

Despite growing financial-assistance problems, no country has as good an all-around higher-educational system as the United States. We try to make postsecondary education available to all strata of society — somewhat inadequately — and we provide more choices for the student than does any other nation.

That does not mean that there are no weaknesses; there are. There are some serious problems facing us. But they have changed significantly since 1958, when the president of the University of California commented: "I find the three administrative problems on a campus are sex for the students, athletics for the alumni, and parking for the faculty."[3]

The Reagan budget, as originally proposed, would have devastated higher education, denying college opportunities to as many as three million American young people and demolishing a good portion of private higher education. Fortunately, there were enough level-headed people of both parties on key committees in the House and Senate that, although some students have been denied the opportunity for college, the damage has been minimized.

But the conscious downgrading of a federal role in education has taken place at all levels, and unless state governments fill the gap — which does not appear likely — history will judge this as a significant step backward for the nation. Yes, you can save money by providing less help to students who need it to go to college, but in the long run that is costly. Yes, you can save money by providing less help for education for the handicapped, but in the long run you deny people the chance to be productive; you add them to the nation's welfare rolls. The litany goes on and on. While Japan, West Germany, the Soviet Union, and many other countries place an increasing emphasis on the importance of education to the future of their countries, we blithely ignore their example, believing we can better prepare our nation for tomorrow with fewer scientists and engineers and social workers.

The damage done to higher education by the Reagan budget cuts is compounded by a reality from the census figures: there will be a decline in our population of 23.3 percent in the eighteen- to twenty-four-year age group by 1997. That means gradually declining enrollments, resulting in some significant financial problems for most colleges and universities.

Particularly hard hit will be the private colleges, with more than one hundred disappearing in the last decade and a larger number probably doomed in this decade. In 1950 half of those attending college in the nation were at private schools; that figure is now one-fifth. The great growth during that period was experienced by the community colleges, which have made a stunning contribution to the nation.

But the private colleges are not alone in facing problems because of declining enrollments. As numbers decline, state legislative bodies may be less willing to vote sufficient funds for public colleges. Faculties will shrink, but those with tenure tend to be the older teachers, and they receive higher pay, so costs per student are likely to rise, and the new ideas and new blood each school needs will decline.

The nation also has a serious curriculum problem that must involve the federal government in its solution. We face a substantial national deficiency of people with foreign-language skills. Admiral Bobby Inman, deputy director of the CIA, has called the failure of our schools to develop people with foreign-language knowledge "a major long-range hazard to the security of the country."[4] It is that and much more, for it deprives us of trade opportunities, too often resulting in our being uninformed about technical developments affecting everything from medical advances to the manufacture of tires. We have both a quantity and quality problem. The chief executive of the Jesuit Colleges in the United States correctly assessed the situation when he wrote: "You can hear more fluent Spanish spoken in a Pan

American 747 than in a university department office."[5] Our deficiencies in language restrict our potential in every area, but in national security these deficiencies can lead to international misunderstandings and literally to calamity.

What should be done in higher education?

Every student, parent, teacher, and school counselor should understand — with considerably less confusion — that anyone who has the ability and wants to go to college should be able to. That in theory is the case now, but students get so much confusing information on what is available that, if they are turned down under one program, they often give up. Under the leadership of Representative William Ford of Michigan and Senator Claiborne Pell of Rhode Island, the Middle Income Student Assistance Act in 1978 established eligibility for student loans. There were some abuses, most of which were quickly corrected, but it is interesting that so many applied who would have been eligible under the old program but had not realized it. Student enrollments grew, and the nation will be richer for generations to come because of that short-lived experiment — "short-lived" because there is now a $30,000 income cap on the loans. In theory I do not disagree with that cap, except that it causes more paperwork; it means that fewer banks will participate in the loan programs because the banks are not in love with the student-loan program anyway, particularly if there is more paperwork and regulation, and that will mean more students getting turned down; and it raises one more question and complication for students and potential students. I have talked to university officials who are badly informed about the student-grant and loan programs. Is it any wonder that an inner-city or rural student gets confused? Our programs need to be simplified to make clear to everyone that college is not only for the economically fortunate.

We should be moving gradually toward something similar to the old GI Bill of the post–World War II years, only not limiting the benefits to veterans. Because the nation thought it should do something for veterans, Congress passed the Servicemen's Readjustment Act of 1944, known as the GI Bill. In a move of generosity (we thought), we provided tuition plus some living expenses to every veteran who wanted to go to college. That generous gift turned out to be one of the best investments this nation ever made. We opened the doors of college to hundreds of thousands of veterans who otherwise never would have attended, and it is estimated that the return to the taxpayers in increased taxes on greater earnings is more than six dollars for every dollar we provided. When we do something generous as a nation, it often serves us better than many things we calculate carefully. (The Marshall Plan after World War II is another such example. It was supported by the people of this nation — if not all of the leaders — not to stop communism or to increase future trade, but because we saw Western Europe in shambles and we felt we should help. It accomplished the other goals also.)

We cannot move into a GI Bill type of program in one fell swoop; right now we are struggling with the administration just to hold onto the student-aid programs we already have. But within two years it will become apparent that our colleges and universities are hurting. Most members of Congress are alumni of those schools. The president of Eureka College will be appealing to President Reagan. College faculty members are increasingly articulate politically, and those business leaders who add dignity to board-of-trustees meetings know how to get things done in Washington. Hurting higher education is not the same politically as hurting food-stamp recipients!

We have a program called the Pell Grant, formerly the Basic Educational Opportunity Grant. On the basis of need, students who qualify may receive grants up to $1,800 per student, to pay up to 50 percent of the costs of college. For three years we have had no increase in allowable costs, while inflation has increased. The Pell program could be modified gradually to become similar to the GI Bill. And we would become a richer nation in the process.

If you go to college in Great Britain or Germany or Japan or almost any other country, your tuition is paid for by the government and you are given a small living stipend. The weakness of the educational program in many of these countries is that it is much more difficult to acquire that collegiate status than it is in the United States. Under the GI Bill, if you did not maintain a certain grade level, you were dropped. That is the screening process I prefer in an open society.

Would this modern version of the GI Bill be costly? Of course it would be, just as the GI Bill was. But are we as generous and wise today as we were in the 1940s? Will we learn from our own history?

Colleges should increase their endowments. The two keys to survival for many small colleges are the maintenance of quality and the size of the endowment. An endowment provides needed income in the event of a real crunch and the flexibility for the increments that can really make the difference between schooling and a rich educational experience. State universities should have endowments too, not that they are threatened with extinction. An endowment permits a school to attract an academic "star" for a semester without fear of the faculty revolting or the governor or state legislature burning a school president in effigy. Our academic priorities become clearer when we recognize that on many campuses it is acceptable to pay the football coach far above the top faculty salary, but if the same wage were paid to a chemistry or journalism teacher, the school's trustees would call for the college president's scalp. To attract a Buckminster Fuller or a Theodore White or a Mary McGrory to a campus for a semester ordinarily will take well above average faculty pay, and an endowment makes that possible without screams from the faculty or trustees or legislature. I have seen endowments make a huge difference in the intellectual climate of a campus. How the federal government can encourage schools to build endowments and individuals and corporations to donate to them is no simple matter. Hearings will be held in Congress on this question. It is not the kind of issue that will attract crowded hearings, television coverage, or pickets, but it is a significant aspect of higher education, both for survival and quality.

The foreign-language crisis — I hesitate to use the word crisis, *but it is an accurate description — must be met by the federal government letting schools at all levels know that this is a national concern.* Traditionally, we have left curriculum to state and local authorities; but unless there is some indication from the federal government of a national need, how can a college president in Nebraska or a school-board member in Illinois know the need exists? In the past the federal government has conveyed that message most effectively by offering a small financial incentive to schools that offer certain courses; vocational education courses are an example of one target of such federal stimulus. American education cannot be insulated from the rest of the world at a time of growing interdependence.

Within the next five years, some type of military/universal service draft is probable. (See Chapter Thirteen.) It is not likely to include the much-abused student deferment of the Vietnam period. If the colleges and federal government plan carefully for that well in advance, it need not be a problem for schools, but rather can turn into an asset, both for students and campuses. Unless there is careful planning, it could aggravate the already mounting enrollment difficulties colleges face.

The research capacity of universities must be maintained. It is important for the research itself and it is important for the training it provides graduate and undergraduate students. It can help with our quality problem. For this nation to slip in basic research — as we have — is a bad omen for the future. The libraries of the nation are an essential part of that research capacity. As dollars become scarce, it becomes all too easy to neglect this vital resource. To neglect either research or libraries in our higher-education community is a great disservice to the nation.

Secondary and Elementary Education

Various indices suggest all is not right with the basic years of education.

In the last six years, averages on the verbal portion of the Scholastic Aptitude Test have dropped from 478 to 427, and the mathematical scores have declined from 502 to 467. Many high-school graduates cannot read or write at the third-grade level. Urban teachers all too often describe their jobs in terms of survival rather than education. Private schools of varying merit are emerging in many communities, sometimes for racial or religious reasons, sometimes because parents have concerns about drugs in the public schools, and sometimes because parents regard the public schools as academically weak.

Little things tell a story, like the high-school foreign-exchange student in our family's home who tells us that in Uruguay high-school students are required to work much harder.

There is another side to the story, however. American schools have moved away from educating only the easy-to-educate and now bring everyone into the system. In another era, if the Swedish immigrant dropped out after the third grade, no one seemed concerned. There were jobs for people with no skills and a third-grade education. But today it is a different world for education and for job opportunities. The discipline-problem student is no longer ejected easily. And broken homes sometimes make a difference in school results. The traditional two-parent family, with one parent working and one at home available to help with schoolwork, is now typical for less than half of the nation's schoolchildren.

For whatever reasons — good and bad — we have to focus on brick-by-brick solutions, rather than look for someone with a magic wand who will suddenly and dramatically change the situation. And most of the solutions are not federal.

What should we be doing?

The most essential ingredient for a good education is a good teacher. A study on foreign-language teaching, for example, found that all of the audio-visual aids made relatively little difference; when students had a good teacher without visual aids, students did well; and when they had a poor teacher with the extras, they did poorly. But the news about teachers is not good. The Scholastic Aptitude Tests show that in eight years there has been a decline of seventy-nine points in the verbal test scores of those who would be teachers. Among all the professions, teacher candidates now rank at the very bottom of SAT verbal and mathematics tests. In addition, many of the finest teachers are leaving for other professions. A survey of all North Carolina teachers between 1973 and 1980 found that two-thirds of those in the bottom 10 percent of test scores were still teaching after seven years, but only one-third of those in the top 10 percent were still teaching. There are some indications of the same trend at the collegiate level. To encourage and attract and keep good teachers, we should:

• Pay teachers adequately. Too often we lose good instructors because they have children in college, or steep mortgage payments. This is particularly true of women faculty members, formerly confined by our culture to limited professional opportunities. They find themselves in a rapidly changing culture, which is more willing to accept women as business executives, engineers, and editors. If the difference in pay between the teaching profession and some alternative is too great, education often loses. Teachers today average thirty-seven years of age, have taught eight years, and for a nine-month year earn $11,800 at the elementary level and $12,196 at the high-school level. That must increase substantially.

• Encourage teachers to continue learning. Teacher "burnout" is real. Colleges have sabbatical programs, and for elementary and high schools that can afford it — and many can — such a program could improve the educational product. Or if traditional sabbaticals are too expensive, a school might occasionally pay a science teacher, for example, to attend a week-long meeting of science teachers during the summer months. Teachers need to be recharged, and most school districts do not recognize this. Teachers also can be encouraged to learn from each other. The school librarian can be instructed to photocopy items he or she thinks might be of interest to specific faculty members; teachers can be encouraged to meet occasionally for breakfast or for an evening in someone's home to discuss a subject; or instructors could gather at the school once every three weeks to hear one of their number talk about something special that is happening, or perhaps to hear a teacher from a neighboring district.

• Give teachers incentives. What if in each high school and each elementary school the teachers voted among themselves for a "teacher of the year" and that teacher received money for a three-week trip abroad the next summer, the only stipulation being that the part of the world visited differ from year to year? It would give meaningful recognition; and it would improve the educational product at that school, for the teacher could tell all of the classes about the visit. In addition, there would be the personal enrichment reflected in that instructor's classroom. For most schools this would cost less than 1 percent of the budget, and what a well-spent 1 percent that would be. Another incentive I would like to see tried by a few school districts on an experimental basis is a system of ranking similar to that on the college level: professor, assistant professor, instructor, or whatever titles might be devised. Teachers justifiably complain that the best teacher in a school system gets paid the same as the worst teacher; that discourages the better teachers and reduces incentives for the weaker teachers. A carefully devised system that rewards excellence has worked well at the collegiate level. It is worth experimenting to see if it would work at the elementary and high-school level. The end result should not be reduced pay for anyone, but rather a higher pay scale and status for some, encouraging better teachers to stay in the profession.

• Encourage colleges to screen students more carefully who want to become teachers. Although test scores do not measure such qualities as enthusiasm and concern, they should still be weighed carefully. Unfortunately, these scores are not encouraging. Someone who wishes to be a chiropodist in Illinois is screened carefully, both to get into a college of chiropody and to get into the profession. I do not want an incompetent examining my feet. But Illinois is much more careful about who handles my feet than about who teaches my children.

• Structure settings that encourage teachers and parents to meet and discuss school problems. One of the good things the program for handicapped education has done is to require an individual plan for each student, bringing the teacher and parents together. Such contacts do not guarantee a better educational product, but dialogue is usually helpful.

Make some form of limited federal per-capita assistance for general use. The suburban schools generally do not need this, but many urban and rural schools do. I talked recently to an English teacher in a small rural school district that is taxing itself to the legal limit. She had to wait seven months to get shades in her classroom so she could show some films she felt were important for her students; she had to pay for the films herself and borrow a film projector from a nearby community college. She is a good, dedicated teacher and she is willing to sacrifice and hassle administrators to get what she feels she needs. But this wealthy nation ought to have a few dollars it can grant without forcing that school district to fill out twenty-two forms. Even a small amount of revenue-sharing type of assistance could mean much to many of these schools. One of the advantages of our present revenue-sharing program with local governments is that it provides revenue with a minimum of paperwork. If we were to include education, we would permit school districts to meet their problems more imaginatively, and do it with less well-intentioned but burdensome regulation and paperwork.

Such funding could permit urban districts in particular to deal creatively with some of their problems. Cincinnati has created three language-magnet schools, one each for French, German, and Spanish. The student population in Cincinnati is approximately half white and half black, and these three schools follow that ratio. I visited all three. It is an exciting thing to walk into an aged school building in a none-too-attractive section of that city, enter a fourth-grade classroom, and watch a multiracial student body get a biology lesson — in German! Not surprisingly, there is a waiting list to get into this school, which people formerly fled.

City and suburban schools will have to work together on such things much more or many cities will find themselves unable to solve problems that eventually spill over into the suburbs. Drugs were a problem first in the ghetto; suburbs and rural areas paid little attention to the drug scene. But yesterday's ghetto problem is today's suburban and rural-district problem. Unfortunately, there is a reluctance on the part of people who have fled the city to join in solving city problems. That must take place. The schools could voluntarily do much more working together than the courts will ever mandate, and do it more effectively.

A small amount of seed money for urban-suburban cooperation could serve the schools well.

School districts with substantial numbers of non-Cuban Hispanics need to develop programs to discourage dropouts and encourage development of students' potential. Cubans do not have a high drop-out rate, but Chicanos and Puerto Ricans do, and far too many schools are doing nothing about it. (The high drop-out rate among Puerto Ricans also indicates a more serious problem that spills over into education and other social problems. The second-class citizenship in which the island finds itself with commonwealth status means that the mainland can with political safety ignore them. Would the Reagan administration have cut back so severely on food stamps in Puerto Rico if the island had a voice in the presidential election and two senators and members in the House? Of course not! Commonwealth status will eventually disappear and be replaced by either independence or statehood. My own opinion is that Puerto Rico and the United States would be much better off with statehood, but that is a decision the Puerto Ricans must first make.)

The nation took a major step forward when it mandated that all handicapped young people must be given the chance to achieve their potential through education, but financial support of that thrust is inadequate. As one who has had a role in the enactment of this law, and its aftermath, I find it exciting.

When hearings were held on the law that requires education for the handicapped, one of those who testified was Ed Akerley, a fourteen-year-old autistic boy. He took special education and then went to the regular school. He told his story in somewhat halting language and was one of the most impressive witnesses I have ever heard. Before educational opportunities came his way, he literally could not put two words together. The record of that hearing includes this exchange:

MR. SIMON: Ed, may I ask you one final question? What would you like to become ten years from now, twenty years from now? What would you like to be doing?

MR. AKERLEY: You mean like when I grow up?

MR. SIMON: That is right.

MR. AKERLEY: Whenever I am out of high school I want to get a good job and get married. When I have my own house I want to have some children and I want to have a dog and a vegetable garden in my backyard.

MR. SIMON: That sounds marvelous. And what do you want to do to make a living to pay for the schooling of those children and buy the vegetable seeds?

MR. AKERLEY: In my vegetable garden I would grow carrot sticks and green peppers and tomatoes.

MR. SIMON: What kind of a job would you like?

MR. AKERLEY: Maybe fixing street lights in an orange snorkel truck before they burn out.

MR. SIMON: You have things pretty well thought out, I tell you that.[6]

I find his story an inspiration — and I cannot believe that thoughtful Americans of either political party can seriously want to cut back on educational opportunities for people like Ed Akerley. School districts were reluctant to accept the responsibility for educating the handicapped, but Congress said that we would gradually increase their funding level if they did. By 1982, the authorizing legislation says, local schools can receive 40 percent of the costs for handicapped children, which on the average are double the costs for the nonhandicapped. And even though the Reagan slash in funding for the handicapped program was not accepted completely, we are still funding at only a 12-percent level. Many school districts simply do not have the funds to do what they know is best for these important young people. School administrators feel that they were given a promise and have been betrayed. The federal budget cannot move immediately to the promised 40 percent level, but we ought to be doing better than 12 percent. If I could only get every member of Congress to see some of the young people I have seen, and what they have done, there would be no question about funding.

Vocational and adult education need greater encouragement and support. Employment statistics on those who have taken vocational-education programs are an effective rebuttal to its critics, although some of the programs do train students for yesterday's demands, rather than today's and tomorrow's. Obsolescence is a danger for individuals in any profession, and it is a danger in education; it is like cancer, spreading silently with fatal results. A quiet, gradual explosion is taking place in education in the increasing numbers of adults who are signing up in courses to update skills, to receive the education they always wanted, or simply to enrich themselves. The Reagan administration ignores the merits of both programs. Both are good and have the potential to contribute much more to the nation. Particularly since the Comprehensive Employment Training Act (CETA) program has been virtually destroyed by the Reagan budget, both vocational and adult-education programs of the more conventional variety should be examined to see if they can meet what will be a growing national employment need. We know that such training increases employability and earnings, and that means both lives and tax dollars salvaged.

School lunches are not an invention of the Kremlin! The Reagan budget reduced the taxes to the nation's wealthiest from 70 percent to 50 percent (few of whom pay either figure) and partially compensated for that by substantially reducing assistance for school lunches. How proud they must be of such an achievement! For hundreds of thousands of young people — perhaps millions — the best meal they receive each day is their school lunch. The Reagan program sounds good: needy children continue to receive the lunches but others pay their own way. The only problem with that is that if those others decide to get McDonald's hamburgers instead or bring their lunches from home, many school districts will find demand too low to continue the program, and school-lunch programs — which have a direct educational effect on many children — often will disappear. That is happening already. In Wisconsin, forty-four school districts have dropped school lunches. In southern Illinois, up to 40 percent of the students are dropping out of school lunches, and many schools will soon drop the program. Democrats should gently remind parents of schoolchildren that what they are paying in increased costs for school lunches in most cases will in and of itself cost more than the tax cut they have received. As one man told me: "The Reagan administration has given me the chance to live in a more expensive neighborhood, and I haven't even had to leave home."

Some of these ideas cost money at all levels of government. But not moving with greater investment in the nation's future will cost even more in the long run. "There is no free lunch," is a phrase heard over and over to describe government programs. That is true. The nation has to determine what our priorities are, and any rational analysis of this nation's needs suggests substantial improvements must yet be made in education and should be a top priority. James Madison put it accurately: "A people who mean to be their own Governors, must arm themselves with the power which knowledge gives."[7]

One major education expenditure should not be enacted: tuition tax credits. This idea, advanced through the years by many respected people and the platforms of both political parties, has several flaws: (1) It is probably unconstitutional to provide assistance to private, largely church-related schools that is not provided to public schools. (2) It reverses the theme of all federal assistance programs in education up to this point: those with the greatest need have priority. The individuals who will benefit the most under tuition tax credits will be those with the greatest income. The parents who struggle to pay tuition to a Catholic or Lutheran or Baptist or Jewish school who do not earn enough money to pay income tax get no relief whatsoever. (3) There is a serious question whether it would really be of help to the private schools because they benefit, at best, indirectly.

The nonpublic schools do need help, but it should be tailored carefully to meet the genuine needs and the constitutional requirements.

Almost all education in the United States was provided originally by the religiously affiliated schools. And the issue of what type of government support should be available has been a thorny, delicate issue since early in the nineteenth century when Roman Catholic Bishop John Hughes of New York City offered to place the Catholic schools under the jurisdiction of what was then the equivalent of the public-school board if the Catholic schools could receive public funding. The Republican platform of 1876 called for a constitutional amendment prohibiting *any* public funds going to parochial schools.

Part of the problem goes to the phrase "separation of church and state," which is not in the Constitution. Thomas Jefferson in one letter talked about "a wall of separation" between church and state, but there has never been any absolute separation. When the Methodist Church is on fire, the fire department is called. No one shouts,

"Separation of church and state! We can't call out the fire department." It is done on the basis that the same service is available to any and all churches or synagogues that are aflame and that it is in the interest of the general welfare to provide assistance. The courts have fairly consistently ruled against tax money that violates either of those principles or that makes public funds available only to churches or church-related schools.

Does that mean that no assistance is possible?

No. At the collegiate level a great deal of assistance is now available both directly and indirectly through aid to students. As I have made clear, I believe that assistance should grow. At the elementary and secondary levels the problems become more difficult, but money in the form of school-lunch assistance, transportation assistance, special programs for the handicapped, driver education, and many other programs can constitutionally be provided to the private-school children and should be. Unfortunately, our maze of regulations sometimes makes that difficult; that can be straightened out without congressional action. In addition, some type of federal per-capita grant to schools, which I advocated earlier in this chapter, could be available to all schools, public and private, so long as they are either recognized or accredited by the state educational agency and its mechanisms, so that we avoid aid to every half dozen parents who want to start a school. We also should not help schools that discriminate on the basis of race — the White Citizens Council type of school. Even the aid suggested here would be taken to the courts and might be ruled unconstitutional, though it stands a much better chance of approval than tuition tax credits — intended solely for the private schools.

The pluralism that is part of the American educational scene must be preserved. Everyone benefits. But it should be done in ways that satisfy both our Constitution and our traditions.

CHAPTER NINE

Culture and Religion

W hen the plea went to Congress for funding for the arts portion of the Works Progress Administration (WPA) in the 1930s, one congressman responded: "Culture? What the hell; let 'em have a pick and shovel!"[1]

That took place more than forty years ago, but the climate has not changed appreciably. That congressman would not share Thomas Jefferson's enthusiasm for the arts: "It is an enthusiasm of which I am not ashamed, as its object is to improve the taste of my countrymen, to increase their reputation, to reconcile to them the respect of the world and to procure them its praise."[2]

Although there is widespread, not deep, backing for assistance to the arts and humanities, sometimes support is lacking because a question of taste is involved. The arts are an easy target. Of the total WPA expenditures in the 1930s, less than 1 percent went for culturally related projects, yet these projects received a high percentage of the criticism leveled at the WPA. It is always easy to find a piece of work that is an evocation of great beauty to some but nothing more than an expression of idiocy to others. Through the perspective of time, however, we know that those dollars were among the finest the federal government ever spent. Many who have dominated the world of music, sculpture, painting, and letters in the last three decades received their initial encouragement from WPA employment. One of the most moving experiences of my elementary years was reading *Black Boy* by Richard Wright. Years later I learned that I had that rich experience because Richard Wright had received encouragement as part of a WPA project.

We now smile knowingly at the foolishness of the critics of yesterday — but we listen to similar criticism today and sometimes let it set policy. The years have not added wisdom to such critics' words; the message they recite is the same. The need is still here; only the time and place have changed.

When the WPA project began, there were eleven recognized symphony orchestras in the United States; the WPA helped to create thirty-four more. In rural and impoverished southern Illinois, symphony orchestras were heard and bands developed. The same thing happened in West Virginia and Kentucky and all across the nation. Print makers encouraged by the WPA experimented with new techniques that drastically altered the graphic-arts industry in the United States and the world. Out-of-work poster artists were employed and "provided 1.6 million posters from 30,500 original designs. These posters promoted fire prevention, prenatal care, noise abatement, better housing, the reading of books, treatment of venereal disease, good nutrition, consumer interests, and a thousand other good causes."[3] The WPA arts projects had spawned "the great flowering of postwar American art."[4]

Where do we stand today? In fiscal year 1981 the federal government spent $0.70 per man, woman, and child for the National Endowment for the Arts (NEA), and President Reagan asked to reduce that to $0.35 in fiscal year 1982. Congress effected a compromise at $0.53. By comparison, Japan spends $1.50 per capita, Canada $6.07, Australia $2.15, Great Britain $3.60, France $11.88, Denmark $28.23, and Austria $100. Austria's capital city of Vienna spends an additional $80 per capita.

The Reagan administration called for a 50-percent cut in expenditures for both the National Endowment for the Arts and the National Endowment for the Humanities (NEH) and for eliminating all federal support for museums. Fortunately, there were enough of us in both parties to stop that wholesale slaughter, but in a year of more than 10-percent inflation, these endowments have been cut back an average of 25 percent. The museum program has been temporarily salvaged, but at a lower support figure.

One of the ironies of these massive cut requests is that the defense function received more than a $40-billion increase, while NEH, the principal funder for our exchanges with the Soviet Union and Eastern Europe, was to be cut in half. More weapons and less

John Mitchell died he left money for a museum, probably as fine a small-town museum as exists in the nation. People who are considering Mt. Vernon as an industrial site are shown the museum and are impressed. It quietly says: "This town has a cultural dimension to it." That museum is an economic plus. Museums are also educational tools of immense power, places where we preserve our heritage. The small Lithuanian museum in Chicago, the Danish museum to be built at Dana College in Nebraska, the thousands of county and city historical museums around the nation — all help to tell us about our roots and can tell future generations the same. But the preservation costs alone are substantial for the great museums. They must keep temperature at a certain level or the great works of art or other items stored will deteriorate. The Reagan attempt to wipe out the museum appropriation failed. We will spend $9.6 million in 1982, or about four cents per man, woman, and child in this country. Is that an extravagant amount to help preserve our heritage?

The arts do more than bring in money. Obviously, one of the reasons Austria spends so much on the arts is to attract tourist dollars, but anyone who has visited that country knows that it does much more than that. It enriches the country in ways that cannot be measured. Austria is not alone in being enriched by the arts in ways that cannot be measured. In Richmond, Virginia, a city that is half black and half white and has a history of racial tensions, the National Endowment for the Arts agreed to provide $5,000 seed money for a three-day downtown arts festival. The June Jubilee was born. Local people added $40,000 to the $5,000 NEA money and for three years in June 200,000 people have visited downtown Richmond at night. In three years, with a tremendous crowd in that small area, there has not been one single incident of racial trouble or crime. Richmond's Mayor Henry Marsh understandably describes the arts as "a unifying force and tremendous asset to our community."[9]

Music, like theater, does not grow on trees. Ellen Shades, who sings with the Metropolitan Opera in New York, got her start from an opera company and school supported by the National Endowment for the Arts. Her story is not unusual, but unless we encourage all of the Ellen Shadeses in this nation, our few opera halls will be filled with those from other countries, not because we do not have the talent, but because we were too shortsighted and disinterested to use it.

Part of my army years was spent in Coburg, Germany, a community of about forty thousand people. Coburg had a professional orchestra and a professional opera company. They simply assumed that a town of forty thousand has those things. We assume the opposite. In East Germany alone, which is about the size of New York, there are sixty year-round opera companies. The United States has none. The Metropolitan Opera Association of New York is approaching it now.

A remarkable book that probably has had minimal sales is *National Theaters in the Larger German and Austrian Cities,* written by Wallace Dace, a professor at Kansas State University.[10] Among other things, Dace looks at the finances of theaters from Linz, Austria (population 205,600), to West Berlin (population two million). All show a heavy government subsidy, 81 percent for Linz and 85 percent for Berlin. The world-recognized Stuttgart Ballet is part of a theater operation that receives an 80-percent subsidy. One of the final chapters in Dace's book is about American singers in Germany and Austria. Lesley Manning-Borchers from Normal, Illinois, comments: "I wanted steady employment as an opera singer. . . . Germany is the place for steady work. And I began in Heidelberg for two years, moved up to Bonn for one year and am now in Wuppertal on a two-year contract. . . . I sing two or three nights a week and sometimes have a stretch of a week without performances. My worst month was fourteen performances. Ideal is about eight performances a month along with all the daytime rehearsals. . . . It is more of a possibility in Europe to have a career and a family, since you can stay put in one place and have a middle-sized career here. In America it has to be career all the way because of the scarcity of [opera] houses and the extreme competition."[11]

Donald Grobe of Ottawa, Illinois, notes that, although he had to work hard on the German language, he has steady employment and makes about $120,000 a year. With a touch of bitterness he adds: "It's a strange country that will subsidize everything from moon shots to farmers not growing things on their land, but will not support its own talent in the fine arts."[12] Baritone William Murray voices a complaint his fellow citizens singing in Europe echo: "The American colleges need to offer more language training to voice students than they do now."[13] (H. L. Mencken once commented, less than accurately:

"Opera in English is just about as sensible as baseball in Italian.")[14] James King, who sings with the Vienna State Opera, shares the bitter feeling of many: "I made my Met debut in December, 1965, as Florestan in *Fidelio,* then returned to my home base over here. I don't get to America very often, but when I do I feel depressed at the lack of the great life-affirming instincts that earlier brought our country to great strength. . . . America seems to be drying up, growing more and more shallow, like a river two feet deep and a mile wide at the mouth. . . . Pop music rules the media because it makes money and that seems to hold the honored position. I'm not against rock, or pop, or disco — just the monopoly of the media by this musical style, much of it dreadful trash, ludicrous, pornographic, promoting degeneracy. I've often said that we can't live constantly in the presence of defecation without eventually smelling of it."[15] The conclusion of the Dace book is that the United States' culture will continue to be handicapped severely until we recognize that the performing arts must receive appreciably more government support than they do now.

Jacob Druckman, a composer, describes the structure of the U.S. musical institutions: "American musical institutions can be compared to a huge pyramid. At the top are the few giants, the half dozen finest orchestras, the three or four great opera houses; just below them, the near giants; and below them, many levels descending to organizations of only regional or community interest. . . . Towards the bottom we find the roots which feed the entire system. Here is the proving ground and training ground. . . . If the NEA suffers considerable cuts, the entire structure will be shaken. . . . At the bottom, where there is absolutely no fat to cut, many will go under."[16]

Many do go under, not only in the field of music, but also in other areas. Presidential papers that should be published are not. Buildings that should be preserved are demolished. Small historical museums that contribute so much too often flounder and fold. Poets often write for themselves. As one observer commented: "A publisher of today would as soon see a burglar in his office as a poet."[17]

The National Endowment for the Humanities helped fund the thirteen-part dramatic series on public television "The Adams Chronicles"; it won an Emmy award. NEH is now helping to fund a documentary on the life of Carl Sandburg. Films of this kind also help to preserve our heritage and enrich us. Do we simply let projects such as these die?

The obvious answer is that we must not. Our total funding for the arts and humanities and museums represents less than a thirty-fifth of 1 percent of the federal budget. These areas should be encouraged to grow and expand so that we become a richer nation, not a poorer nation. "They had no poets, so the city died," is an old Chinese description of one of its ancient cities. The double irony of the present struggle to maintain the status quo is that the endowments have been dramatically successful in measurable terms. When the NEA started in 1965, there were 7 state arts councils and only a handful of local councils. Now every state has one and there are more than 2,300 local councils. Every form of art has grown. In 1965 there were 7 professional resident theater companies in the nation and now there are 65. In 1965 there were 58 professional symphony orchestras in the nation and in 1980 there were 144. In the past ten years the numbers of concerts has grown from 5,000 to more than 16,000. A 1980 Lou Harris poll shows a dramatic increase in participation in the arts since 1975, when their last poll on this subject was taken. The number of people singing in a choir has almost doubled; the number who participate in dance of some form has more than doubled; those playing musical instruments has grown from 18 to 30 percent. Attendance at museums, plays, and classical musical events is up markedly. And in support of the arts the people are ahead of the politicians. The 1980 poll showed that the public would support, by a margin of 59 to 39 percent, $15 more per capita in taxes to fund the arts; in 1975 they opposed this 50 to 46 percent. At $5 this margin grows to 70 to 28 percent for support — and that is approximately nine times the present level of support.[18]

When we eventually return to a sensible job-creating policy on the part of the federal government (see Chapter Five), part of it should be devoted to encouraging orchestras and choruses and opera companies and writers and artists and historians — people who, though often controversial, add vision and dimension to life in this nation. These groups and individuals reach children and adults in communities untouched by such opportunities now except through radio and television. Almost two thousand years ago Ovid wrote: "Nothing is more useful to man than those arts which have no utility."[19] How accurate is this seeming contradiction!

In so many little ways we are discouraging cultural enrichment rather than encouraging it. And it is not the endowments alone. The difficulties that higher education faces will have a major impact on the arts and the humanities. College presidents will have to ask themselves: How important is the university orchestra? Can we continue to subsidize a university museum? Can we cut back on library acquisitions?

The cultural isolation of the United States is also a problem. When the hostages were taken in Iran I found myself reading about Shiite Moslems and Sunni Moslems, and even though I have visited a number of Moslem countries through the years, I suddenly realized that I knew little of the beliefs of the people of that massive part of the world. Even when public television does a series on the history of civilization, it confines that study to Western Europe and North America. A Japanese official comments in a recent publication: "English language books and magazines are translated into Japanese on a ratio of twenty to one book or magazine translated from Japanese into English. . . . This is one example of the communication gap."[20] We must become more open to culture outside of our country as well as within it.

Even such a noncultural appearing arm of the government as the Postal Service weighs heavily. After the restructuring of 1970, we assumed that the new "businesslike" Postal Service could make money. It is an assumption that has plagued all administrations since the beginning of our nation. In fact, if the free flow of ideas is important to this country — and it is — we should not be subsidizing Lockheed and Chrysler while we put small magazines (and some large ones) out of business with increasing postage rates, nor should we be raising first-class rates so high that people I visit in nursing homes are reluctant to write to their relatives. I visited the offices of the *Paducah Sun* and the editor told me that they had to raise subscription rates so high that a good portion of their rural subscribers discontinued the newspaper. Those people are now relying on television and radio for all of their news. Is that what our government policy ought to be? Books are becoming too expensive, and we make people who buy them and libraries that use them pay higher and higher postage rates. The cultural environment of this country ought to keep people as fully informed as possible, about as much as possible, giving every conceivable viewpoint a chance to be heard. Yet we adopt government policies that go in precisely the opposite direction. I do not expect the Defense Department to make money because it is serving a national purpose. And if the Postal Service does not make money because it serves a national purpose I shall shed no tears. Run it efficiently and use common sense in operating it (both factors too frequently missing now), and if we must subsidize it a little more, I'm for it.

An extremely important part of the culture of this country is religion. And occasionally the religious phenomenon crosses that of government in an unusual way. The Know-Nothings of the last century built on religious prejudices. The Ku Klux Klan in a much cruder way has done the same in this century. In 1928 and in 1960 the religious issue dominated the presidential election. The intertwining of religion and government reached a hysterical high point in Jonestown, Guyana, when hundreds committed suicide at the request of a minister-leader with a tortured mind. Now a group that calls itself the Moral Majority has emerged. Political leaders find it awkward to deal with. Like the Klan, this is in part a geographical phenomenon, primarily of great influence in the South and near south. Like the Klan, Moral Majority followers embrace a strange mix of politics, religion, and nostalgia. Unlike the Klan, they operate openly and have no truck with violence. And unlike the Klan, on some issues the group unquestionably voices the opinion of the majority of Americans: for example, there is too much violence on television, a position with which I personally strongly agree. There are millions of Americans who see cable television invading their homes with movies that produce outrage, they see magazines in the corner grocery store that stir anger, and there is an unspoken sense on the part of many that something has gone drastically wrong with our culture and our moorings. Then suddenly there on a television screen in front of them someone says: "Let's do something about this." And they agree. There is, however, as in many religious movements that include political action, a touch of the "holy-war" atmosphere, the group portraying those with differing views in the severest terms, with no recognition that an issue might have another side to it. A former United States senator told a Presbyterian seminary recently that the Moral Majority "needs a healthy dose of humility."[21] Members of the Moral Majority are sincere, well-meaning people. But they are being misled. They tend not to be associated with the mainline Christian churches. I know no Catholic or Lutheran members connected with the Moral Majority, for example, though I know there are some.

Those who say the Moral Majority has no right to get involved in politics do not understand our Constitution. The group is, so far as I know, operating within the law in every respect. They are exercising a constitutional right to be wrong on many issues, from my perspective. But political leaders make a mistake if they go beyond that and suggest the Moral Majority is less than sincere, or that their activity violates some American tradition.

The Moral Majority is a political movement wrapped in a veneer of theology and the cloak of Protestant fundamentalism. But a host of Protestant fundamentalists, including Billy Graham, disapprove of their approach. As the son of a Lutheran minister and brother of another, I cannot harmonize what I learned and believe with some of the positions the Moral Majority takes. For example, one of the more famous scenes depicted in the New Testament is in Matthew 25, Judgment Day, when Christ asks the ultimate questions: "Did you help the hungry, the naked, the sick, and those in prison?" I find the Moral Majority strangely quiet on all of these issues. I have yet to hear from them on the massive problem of world hunger. When I appeared on a television program with a spokesman for the Moral Majority and asked him why they are so audibly silent on such issues as world hunger, he said these are individual responsibilities, not the proper role of government. There is a selective picking and choosing in the Moral Majority's ideas of the proper role of government, and compassion for the poor and desperate of this nation and the world is not evidenced in their positions.

The Christian Voice is a publication that rates members of Congress on the Moral Majority issues. I got a zero, out of a possible one hundred. I know that I am morally imperfect, but I did not understand the extent of my imperfection until that rating came out. Father Robert Drinan, a Catholic priest then a member of Congress, also got a zero, and Reverend Robert Edgar, a Methodist minister who serves in Congress from the Philadelphia area, got only 8 percent. A Republican member of the House, since defeated through Moral Majority efforts, Representative John Buchanan of Alabama, also a Baptist minister, received a 28-percent rating, while

Representative Richard Kelly of Florida, convicted in the Abscam trials of accepting $25,000 in bribe money, received a 100-percent rating. The Moral Majority chose such issues as the establishment of a Department of Education. I regarded it as a structural change with little meaning in and of itself. But mine was called an "immoral" vote. I also voted to provide help to state and local agencies that give shelter to battered wives. That was listed as an antifamily vote. Presumably, part of healthy family life is allowing a husband to make a punching bag out of his wife. The second phase of the Strategic Arms Limitations Talks (SALT II) and the Panama Canal Treaty were also targets of their wrath.

The founder, Reverend Jerry Falwell, did not suddenly emerge on the political scene in 1980. He first attracted attention with his statements denouncing the 1954 Supreme Court decision on desegregation of the schools. In 1958 he said: "If Chief Justice Warren and his associates had known God's word and had desired to do the Lord's will, I am quite confident that the 1954 decision would never have been made. . . . The facilities [for the races] should be separate. When God has drawn a line of distinction, we should not attempt to cross that line."[22] That position has changed, as have some others. In a *Los Angeles Times* interview, Falwell said: "My father was supportive of segregation and so was I, even in the early years of my ministry. It wasn't until I spiritually developed and matured, as I see it, that I came to realize it was an unscriptural position."[23] But a lack of sensitivity to others continues. His New York state office director, Reverend Dan C. Fore, told the *New York Times:* "I love the Jewish people dearly. God has given them talents he has not given others. They are his chosen people. Jews have a God-given ability to make money, almost a supernatural ability to make money."[24] In 1976 Falwell opposed Jimmy Carter, the first "born-again Christian" candidate for president. His position then had little impact. But by 1980 matters changed.

Many of us who consider ourselves Christians, however inadequately we live our faith, are also troubled by the very term "Moral Majority," for it suggests an arrogance, a "Lord we thank thee that we are not as other men are" attitude.

But Falwellites have struck a responsive chord with large numbers of people, convincing them that the thrust of the Democratic party departs from the basic principles upon which the nation was founded.

The Falwellites and their philosophical bedfellows have used issues such as prayer in the schools, wrapping themselves in the flag, suggesting that those who differ with them are leading the nation to ruin. In fact, on this and other issues, those who support the Supreme Court's decision, which simply said there shall be no forced and prescribed prayer in the schools, are the ones going back to the basics. But Democrats have permitted themselves to be painted as irreligious and immoral, as a party representing the fringes of the nation. When the religious far Right says that the nation should get back to the country's basic principles, we should agree and vigorously oppose the characterization of the party that some have promoted. Bad political views wrapped in the name of religion are still bad political views. If Democrats fail to respond to — and persuade — the Falwellites and their counterparts, the Democratic party will be abandoning a large part of its constituency. Ironically, those to whom the Moral Majority has the most appeal tend to be the poor and the lower middle class, the very people who are helped most by Democratic programs. Ours is a party that stands for family, protection, good neighborhoods and schools, and other ideals the Falwell followers hold dear.

Charles Peters, editor of the *Washington Monthly,* comes from West Virginia, which like my district in southern Illinois would be considered Falwell territory. He told of making a speech there recently in which he praised the Democratic party for its "traditional advocacy of programs designed to help the less fortunate. After the speech a woman asked me, 'Who says my husband and I should have to give money we've worked hard for to anyone else? Who says? I just want to know who tells me I have to do that.' 'Madam,' a friend of mine interjected, 'it is your Lord Jesus Christ who tells you.'"[25]

CHAPTER TEN

Agriculture

T he family farm must be placed alongside motherhood, the flag, Boy Scouts, Girl Scouts, and apple pie as sacred cows to which all politicians bow. Yet the family farm — for reasons good and bad — will be an endangered phenomenon soon unless governmental policies change.

Before World War I, 27 percent of all those employed in this country worked at farming. The average farm was 130.5 acres. In 1940, the average farm was 175 acres, in 1950, 213 acres. By 1960, farms averaged more than 300 acres and less than 8 percent of our working population engaged in farm work. Today the average farm is approximately 450 acres and 3.2 percent of our employed population works on farms.

That is only a part of the story. Today 64,000 farms, each with over $200,000 gross income, produce 39.4 percent of the agricultural products of the nation. Those 64,000 farms are 2.4 percent of the total number of farms. The small farms with between $5,000 and $40,000 gross income produce 16.4 percent of the gross sales. There are 898,000 of those small farms. In other words, there are fourteen times as many small farms as those large ones, yet they account for less than half as much food sales.

That is part of the American agricultural revolution.

Farm life is not what it used to be. I did not grow up on a farm, but about half my relatives were farmers and I worked on farms beginning in my grade-school years. Most of those farms did not have electricity. Every farm had at least one cow. We churned butter by hand, hand-cranked a cream and milk separator, and took the milk cans to the road for pick-up with nowhere near the sanitary requirements of today. We salted the meat and kept it in a separate shed to preserve it. Many farmers owned tractors, but many still plowed the fields with horses. Born in 1928, I have seen a revolution in farm living in my lifetime. Today's farm family has access to all the conveniences of city life — if it can afford them.

The technological change is not simply that farms now have refrigerators and electric stoves and television sets. Farm machinery has replaced the horse, and a farmer can ride in an air-conditioned combine listening to stereo music, if the family income permits that. And much more important than these factors, new wheat and soybean and corn strains have increased production tremendously; fertilizers are as different as the jet airplane is different from the Model T Ford; cattle and hogs are bred to produce more and better meat. The other day I visited a hog farm in my district, operated by Wayne Mashoff; he has 2,500 hogs and it is like a factory, with none of the animals setting foot on actual ground from the moment of birth until they are taken to market. America's farmers are producing more food with less people than ever before, and they are the envy of farmers all over the world.

On top of everything else, world population growth and improved incomes gradually will increase demand for food. Even assuming that small farmers in developing nations produce more, world food prices are expected to increase an average of at least 2.5 percent a year above inflation.

What is wrong?

1. While the family farm is an efficient unit for production, the value of most farm acreage has been increasing faster than inflation. Thus, speculators, large corporations, pension funds, foreign companies, and individual Americans find farmland an attractive investment. That sends land values up, does not increase production, and reduces the number of family farms.

2. The average age of farmers is creeping up and is now well past fifty. Farms are sometimes broken up because of inheritance laws (though 1981 changes in these laws should help), and potential young farmers are not buying land because prices are beyond their reach.

3. High interest rates hurt agriculture. A century ago an observer noted: "The Golden Age of the small farmer is over. He can barely get along. He is in debt to the cattle-dealer, the land speculator, the usurer. Mortgages ruin whole communities, even more than taxes."[1] Things have not changed much. Few farmers can operate without

borrowing money. Sometimes it is for fertilizer and seed, sometimes for a new tractor or milking machine, sometimes to repair a barn, and sometimes to tide them over due to a bad crop the year before. But at 17- or 18-percent interest, the farmer often does not earn enough to pay the interest, much less the principal on those loans. And the young couple who would like to buy a farm is ruled out completely by high interest rates, though at least two states now subsidize this type of loan. The average farmer would be much better off financially simply selling the farm and drawing interest on the investment. Fortunately, however, there are many people in our country who like farming as a way of life and do not make decisions solely on a financial basis; but high interest rates are making that more difficult.

4. Farm assistance programs make no distinction between the active farmer who owns and farms his land and the absentee owner who bought the land for speculative purposes or simply for the thrill of saying he owns a farm. That keeps agriculture land prices up and prevents some potential family farms from becoming reality.

5. Agricultural research, in both its orientation and application, tends to help the large farmer rather than the small farmer.

6. The marketing system is geared toward large producers.

7. The nation's transportation system — particularly the railroads — is crumbling and farmers are adversely affected.

8. Farmers have to gamble on the weather, but the volatility of the commodity price level adds immeasurably to their economic woes.

9. We're losing far too much of our topsoil.

10. Highways, new housing subdivisions, and other creations of the modern world are chewing up productive farmland at an alarming rate.

What can be done about all of this?

We should consider the possibility of exempting farmland not owned by operating farmers from the benefits of the capital-gains tax. If that change were made (perhaps exempting all those holding ownership already), farmland would not be such a desirable investment for the nonfarmer and more of those who actually operate the farms could own them. Nonowners who farm have year-to-year uncertainties, which means they do not make the "small" improvements that might pay off over a period of years, such as preventing soil erosion, or the major improvements, such as building a new home or barn.

If there are cash payments or allotments (in peanuts and tobacco), we should study the possibility of restricting them to farmers who own their land. Some years ago (before I served in Congress) my wife and I owned a small farm to which we escaped now and then for relaxation. Occasionally, I received a small government check, under various farm programs. Obviously, that did not discourage absentee ownership. Owners who do not actively farm should not be beneficiaries of these programs. Thirty-five percent of payments go to landowners who do not operate the farm. If they were excluded from the commodity support payments, it would save money and encourage farmer ownership of land. If such a program were to be adopted, it should be combined with a program that helps the operating farmer purchase the land he farms.

Research should be done to benefit small farms. Private research inevitably gravitates toward the large purchaser of the product of that research. That means that when Ralston Purina or any other firm does research it is more likely to be oriented toward, and to benefit, the large-farm operator, though the small family farm often can benefit, too. But publicly supported research should be geared more to the small farmer who needs help, and greater stress should be given to bringing benefits to that farmer. Agricultural research must receive greater emphasis; American agriculture reached its present unbelievable heights of production in great part because of excellent research. The general research must continue, but we need to develop more targeted research for the small-farm operation as well. Great stress has been placed in the past, for example, on labor-saving agricultural research. The need for the small farmer has shifted so that research should take place on capital-saving and energy-saving technologies. Practices that are less chemical-intensive and may require more labor could be of substantial benefit to many small farmers, but might not be of much interest to the large farm operation. Universities should be encouraged in their research to make application of the new seeds or processes to the small-farm operation, not simply the large one. The small farm my wife and I purchased was priced at a relatively low cost per acre, otherwise we could not have afforded to buy it. Not long after we bought it, I called the Soil Conservation Service to ask them to send someone out to look at our place to determine whether we were doing what we should to conserve the soil. He told us: "I don't get many calls in this part of the county. The northern half is where the better soil and wealthier farms are. It's funny when you think about it, because the program was designed for the poorer farmers, but they don't take advantage of it." There are reasons, including the fact that some of those commendable practices cost money and don't pay off for many years. The marginal farmer in the southern part of Fayette County has to struggle year by year to stay afloat and does not have the luxury to plan a long-range soil-conservation program. That flaw in the application of research, and in the research itself, should be corrected.

It is ironic that the world's wealthiest nation is gradually developing the worst railroad transportation system of any major power. Administration officials are seriously talking about passenger service eventually only for the Washington, D.C.-to-Boston area. Conrail is gradually getting out of the business, abandoning many miles of railroad service and abandoning communities and farmers along the way also. Railroad service is gradually deteriorating; if farmers have a good year of corn or beans or wheat or anything else, they may have to dump their product on the ground while they wait for railroad cars. The railroad situation affects more than farmers, but because farmers do not have a choice of when to ship their grain, unless they have storage facilities, they are more severely hurt by deteriorating railroad service than others.

In almost all countries the railroad system is owned by the national government. Instead, we make questionable "loans" to the railroads to keep them at a survival level. Two steps would improve the railroad situation appreciably. First, we should require railroads, as we do utilities, to invest in themselves rather than siphoning off profits to invest in everything from a Pepsi-Cola bottling operation to a pantyhose factory. If the railroads knew that their business was railroading and nothing else, service would improve. Second, the railroad beds of the nation have deteriorated badly, with a few exceptions, such as the Santa Fe. Let the federal government buy the railroad beds from railroads that wish to sell, buying over a period of years, and put some unemployed people to work fixing the beds, and then charge the railroads for the use of them.

Transportation problems that farmers face are not solely rail, however. The nation's rivers and canals must be maintained and ports that handle exports must be prepared for greater grain shipments. In the 1950s exports accounted for 10 percent of marketed farm products; now it is over 30 percent and climbing. Port facilities have become important to the American farmer.

We need to take steps to guard that most basic of resources — land. We do it in part through greater prudence in constructing highways and parking lots and subdivisions. Former Secretary of Agriculture Bob Bergland — one of the better agricultural secretaries this nation has had — says that during his lifetime more good tillable soil has been paved than exists in the entire state of Ohio. We construct highways as if there were an unending source of land from which to grow food. In the past ten years the nation has paved, subdivided for housing, or otherwise consumed agricultural acreage twice the size of New Jersey.

We must guard our land by watching our topsoil much more carefully. Erik Eckholm writes: "Perhaps an even greater threat to future human welfare than the pollution of our air and water is that exacted by the undermining of the land itself through accelerated soil erosion, creeping deserts, increased flooding, and declining soil fertility."[2] The *New York Times* of May 12, 1934 reported: "A cloud of dust thousands of feet high, which came from drought-ridden states as far west as Montana, fifteen hundred miles away, filtered the rays of the sun for five hours yesterday. New York was obscured in a half-light similar to the light cast by the sun in a partial eclipse."[3] Washington, D.C., experienced the same phenomenon. The day before, Chicago had been hit even harder, with an average of four pounds of dust per person. A month earlier, Kansas and eastern Colorado were enveloped by a dust storm so bad that at noon there was total darkness. It killed the birds and rabbits and small animals. That 1934 experience, coming from what became known as the Dust Bowl, signaled the blowing away of much of America's topsoil. Thanks in large part to the efforts of the Soil Conservation Service created one year later, that area of the nation has been salvaged and is productive once again. All over this nation our topsoil is now gradually disappearing, mostly because of water runoff, and once again the wind is also becoming the enemy. Cropland is losing an average of eight tons of topsoil a year; the regenerative process puts back only two to five tons per year. Iowa farmers are now growing soybeans and corn on an average of eight inches of topsoil. Illinois now washes away about two bushels of topsoil for every bushel of corn produced. How long can this continue? In 1975 a distinguished group of experts, the Council for Agricultural Science and Technology, warned that the United States "may be creating another dust bowl."[4] Erosion figures for the major crops are: cotton, 19.9 tons per acre; sorghum, 12.6 tons; soybeans, 8.2 tons; corn, 7.6 tons; and wheat, 6.5 tons. In 1975 the General Accounting Office suggested that to protect the soil the nation should stop cutting down its trees. Trees serve a double purpose, building back the topsoil and preventing flooding that takes it away; not so incidentally, they also help to purify our air. There is a casual, almost fatalistic indifference on the part of many farmers and government officials to this problem of soil erosion. That must change. The nature of our political decision making in the United States tends to be short-range. There are areas where we can tolerate shortsightedness. This is not one of them.

Our commodities programs need to be reshaped. This can be done in a way that will cost the government less and help the small farmer more. Farms with more than $250,000 gross income — that figure could be adjusted — should not be eligible for direct commodity support. They could continue to participate in the reserve program, but they are at a high enough income level so that direct support is unnecessary.

The 1978 farm programs, payments for nonproduction, and other direct support, including disaster payments, had these results: "Ninety percent of the participating farmers had a normal cropland acreage of less than five hundred acres. They received only 54 percent of the payments. The smallest 30 percent of the farmers received less than four percent of the payments. The larger farmers with a normal cropland acreage of five hundred acres or more — 10 percent of all farmers who participated — received 46 percent of the payments."[5] The same report notes: "Most of the basic program mechanisms that are in use were originally developed for treatment of the low-income problem. . . . They provide benefits based on the volume of production, implicitly skewing the distribution of benefits to the large-volume producers."[6] There is an economic as well as an equity reason for restricting assistance because, as a Department of Agriculture report study concludes: "Most of the primary farms have reached or surpassed the size needed to attain most economies related to size. The major portion of our food and fiber is thus produced by farms that are beyond the most technically efficient."[7] All farms should continue to be eligible for disaster loans when that is necessary, but the thrust of the commodity program should be to help the small farmer.

For the smaller farmers commodity payments should be primarily in the form of "target price support," so that the market can operate on its own freely, while farmers are assured the cost of production. It would work this way: if, for example, the cost to produce a bushel of soybeans is determined to be $7.50, and the market price drops to $7.30, then the farmer is paid the difference, or $0.20 per bushel. If the market price is $7.70, the federal government is not out any money. With the anticipated demand on U.S. commodities, payments should be fairly limited but offer a floor for the small farmers who need assistance the most. The advantage of this system is that the consumer benefits, the farmer benefits, and the government benefits. Some modification of this system should apply to sugar, milk, and peanuts, programs that now vary considerably. The tobacco program will continue with us — that is the political reality — but perhaps my lack of enthusiasm is colored by the fact that I have so few tobacco farmers in my district.

The reserve program, though new, can become the fundamental price-stabilizing mechanism. Secretary Bergland called it "the major agricultural policy tool."[8] Interestingly, it came about primarily, not because of lobbying by farm groups, but by a religious group, Bread for the World, which had a concern for stability of price and supply because of the needs of impoverished people in developing nations. Under the reserve program, the government extends loans to farmers, with the grain serving as security. The loan helps farmers meet general farming expenses, also allowing them to hold the grain until prices recover. It is stored on farms or in nearby community elevators. The government provides farmers with an annual payment to help defray storage costs. If grain prices increase, the farmer can pay off the loan and market the grain or hold it longer in the hope of further price improvement. The practical effort of the loan level is to establish a floor for grain prices. If grain prices do not exceed the loan level, farmers can forfeit their grain to the government, keeping the loan proceeds, and they do not have to pay the interest on the loan.

Since prices improve as supplies decrease, farmers hold the grain until prices strengthen, helping to assure that supplies will be adequate in the event of drought or a food emergency. The reserve stabilizes prices, assures a supply of grain, and protects farm income. The benefits of the reserve are related to size, however. If the reserve is too small it will have minimal impact.

Whatever helps agriculture will help small towns, but programs to encourage adequate water and sewer systems and the development of small industry are also helpful. A disproportionately high percentage of those who end up in *Who's Who* and lead the nation are from small communities. It is no disparagement of urban life, which also has its assets, to say that there is something good about small-town America, particularly its feeling of shared concern, which somehow gets lost in urban and suburban areas. But too many small towns have dried up and almost blown away. There is a renewed interest in small towns now, however, as the 1980 census makes clear, aided in large part by senior citizens returning from industrial jobs in urban areas after retirement. In general it is true for rural communities as for urban areas: whatever helps people helps small towns.

Water is going to play a much more important part in agriculture in the future. In some areas of the nation, farmers — and cities — are using below-ground water more rapidly than nature can restore the supply. That is one problem not yet faced, in part because there is disagreement as to the extent of the problem. Demand for protein will result in utilizing small ponds for fish farming, now so rare in the United States it is almost exotic. That will become commonplace. And the great new source for protein will be the ocean, now used primarily as we formerly used land: for food by hunting (only when we "hunt" for fish we call it fishing). But gradually the ocean will be farmed. Mussels, a delicacy in much of Europe, are hard to find even in a seafood restaurant in the United States. But one acre of ocean can grow as much as 260,000 pounds of high-protein mussels every year. That type of sea farming must be experimented with and encouraged.

The miniscule efforts now being made to find an inexpensive process to convert salt water into fresh water should be pushed much more, for when that breakthrough comes — and inevitably it will come — it will change the food map of the world dramatically. And that will help the American farmer. As Israel has made the desert bloom in many places with the right application of water and technology, so the deserts in the United States and elsewhere can bloom. Twenty years after such a breakthrough, Egypt will be a dramatically different, and better, country. The politics of the Middle East will change; prejudices will not change overnight, but one of the causes of irritation will disappear. And in a majority of the earth's nations, including the United States, food productivity will increase, and the specter of severe malnutrition will be haunting fewer of the earth's people.

This research requires a long-term commitment and long-range planning. All government policy making has a tendency to be short-range, meeting an immediate problem, rather than long-range. Nowhere is this more true than in the field of agriculture.

As we pursue these long-range goals we should talk and listen to all of the farm organizations. I confess I was a bit startled when the Farm Bureau, which for many years strongly advocated a balanced budget, came to me lobbying for the Reagan tax cut, which throws the budget far out of balance. Although I am startled by that position, they have good ideas in other areas — on transportation, exports, and other concerns of farmers. So do the Farmers Union, the National Farm Organization, the National Grange, and the more specialized groups such as the Soybean Growers. None of these groups should be ignored; we need to take the best ideas from all of them.

We should ask ourselves more of the basic questions and then define our goals. Ten farmers may want ten different farm programs for today, but most of the ten could agree that we want to encourage the family farm, preserve our soil, and produce more and better food for the people of our country and others. Unfortunately, our day-to-day policy decisions have not meshed with those goals.

CHAPTER ELEVEN

The Cities

" "When we get piled upon one another in large cities, as in Europe, we shall become as corrupt as Europe," Thomas Jefferson wrote to James Madison in 1785.[1] The anticity bias has been popular in this country since before Jefferson's time. Cities tend to magnify virtues and vices, and even as the nation moved to the city, we often did it reluctantly, with a nostalgic look back to a pastoral scene that became inaccurately gilded with the years.

The cities are in serious trouble, although some have started to revive and will continue to do so, not because of but despite the Reagan program. President Reagan's program, among other things, *does* take from the poor and give to the more affluent, and most cities have a much higher percentage of poor than their suburbs, and generally than their rural neighbors as well. However, enough good things have been happening in Detroit, Washington, Baltimore, and other cities to cause stories of optimism and buoyancy. Still, the undergirding statistics for the cities generally continue to be grim. For the truth remains that a disproportionately high percentage of those who have given up hope in our society live in the cities.

Two things the cities do *not* need: more studies and more short-range reorganizational plans. Studies too easily become a substitute for action. East St. Louis, Illinois, for example, literally has been studied almost to death. That city continues to have the highest crime rate of any municipality its size in the nation. And while it now has a mayor, Carl Officer, with substantial leadership potential, unless Illinois someday gets a governor who pays more than lip service to the problems and potential of East St. Louis, the mayor and those who share the leadership face an almost impossible job. What is true of

East St. Louis is true of almost any old, urban area. We've had enough studies; we need action.

The second proposal that emerges time after time is a governmental reorganizational scheme that will immediately salvage a city. I have been in politics long enough to recognize that the only merit such proposals ordinarily have is that they bring new leadership in, which is usually the real object of the "reorganization." A good governmental structure with the wrong people in charge will do poorly; a bad governmental structure with the right people in charge will do well. That is political reality. In 66 A.D. Gaius Petronius wrote: "We tried hard . . . but it seemed every time we were beginning to form up into teams, we were reorganized. I was to learn later in life that we tend to meet any such situation by reorganizing. A wonderful method it can be for creating the illusion of progress while producing confusion, inefficiency, and demoralization."[2] Some things don't change with time. These remarks do not preclude any study or any reorganization, of course, but such suggestions today too often represent an escape from rather than a facing of reality.

There should be *long-range* planning — for the streets, sewers, water and subway systems, and other basic structural services on which a city is built. These wear out eventually, and almost no planning has been done with that day in mind. Houston might well start planning now for that obsolescence, even though it is one of the boom cities of today; it should be pointed out that the first big oil-boom city of the nation was Cleveland. Many urban problems are caused by a common failure of government at all levels: lack of long-range planning. The cities that are not prospering must build such a planning base, and the cities that are thriving must remember that the day when their facilities are all new and in good working order will pass.

The cities historically have represented hope — to people who have fled desperate rural poverty, who have come from other countries and found an ethnic community in which they could feel comfortable, who have wanted to make their mark in the business or professional world, for there has always been more of an aura of prestige to say that you are a lawyer from New York or Chicago than a lawyer from Keokuk, Iowa, or Bonduel, Wisconsin. Cities represent cultural diversity and opportunity as well as hope. But they also represent desperation and fear and lack of community.

The principal benefit the federal government can provide cities is to help people directly. Nothing could help urban areas as much as guaranteeing everyone a chance for a job (see Chapter Five). Cities also benefit from national programs to meet problems of health, education, and transportation. When the nation cleans its air, cities become more livable. When rural areas prosper, there are no mass movements of their poor, who are ill-equipped for urban life, into the cities. Since the problems of the cities are focused particularly on the poor, any federal programs that help impoverished people help urban America. In New York City, for example, 1.2 million people benefit from food stamps, and even though food stamps are calculated on a base of slightly less than forty-five cents per meal, food-stamp assistance is of significant help to the diets and lives of the poor of New York City. For the nation to pretend that it can help cities while neglecting the poor — as the Reagan program does — is like professing great love for children and not feeding them adequately (which the Reagan program also does). But cities have specific needs and opportunities that should be addressed.

There has to be greater sharing between the central city and the suburbs. This is happening to a limited extent in most areas, Indianapolis being probably the best example. The structural merging Indianapolis has achieved is not likely to take place elsewhere. But on a function-by-function basis, greater cooperation can be achieved. For example, every survey of why people leave the central city shows that the number-one reason is the poor quality of the schools, though some of the replies probably hide the true reason: racial attitudes. But deteriorating schools in the cities are a real, not an imagined, problem. Suburban and city schools can work together to establish magnet schools, as one example of possible cooperation. Why shouldn't parents who live in the suburbs be able to send their children to a central-city school that has a heavy foreign-language emphasis? Or a music emphasis? And if a suburban school has an excellent vocational-education program in carpentry, the city schools should be able to work out an exchange. When people hear the word *busing*, fears and emotions erupt; but if programmatic exchanges take place on a voluntary basis, the same — or a better — result can be achieved. This can happen within a city system; but if the city and suburban school districts cooperate, an even finer educational product can be achieved. The enrollment decline in urban and some suburban schools gives leaders with imagination and creativity and courage a chance to do some things that are less than conventional. That creative spark should be nurtured in part by state and federal funds.

Urban housing programs need to encourage rehabilitation rather than destruction. Many old neighborhoods should be salvaged not destroyed. Economic integration must be recognized as fully as important as racial integration, for if the people who don't know how to solve problems are stockpiled on top of people who don't know how to solve problems, not surprisingly, the problems multiply. It is interesting that in small-town America economic integration has taken place without planning for it. The result is that if Mrs. Jones has problems with her husband, who drinks too much, or the Smiths have difficulties because the breadwinner is temporarily out of work, the neighborhood and community are aware of the problems and are more apt to help make life a little more bearable for them. But people who live in the midst of a sea of trouble usually don't have that backup support. High-rise public-housing developments are most successful for the elderly and handicapped. All other high-rise public-housing developments I have seen segregate by economics and are disasters. Housing beyond repair should be torn down; it might be replaced by small park and recreation areas. Cities should have more trees and shuffleboard courts and places to play basketball.

Germany has a practice the United States could well emulate. Under their laws, leases impose on residents the responsibility for maintenance of the appearance of property and landlords are responsible for the basic maintenance. These requirements are strictly enforced. Too often in the United States ownership is by someone who wants to put in nothing for maintenance, looking for either income without effort or a tax write-off, and those who occupy such housing have little respect for what happens to an already badly deteriorated structure.

The Capitol Hill area in Washington, D.C., has gone from an area for wealthy whites to an area for poor blacks and now is gradually reverting to an upper-middle-income neighborhood, integrated but predominately white. But there is little planning for homes or apartments for the poor, here and there, in the midst of the property being upgraded. And what is happening in Washington, D.C., is happening in a few other cities and probably will eventually happen in all. The blacks who leave move to mostly black areas in the suburbs, but areas with school systems generally superior to the District of Columbia school system. As their incomes grow, and as their children graduate from school, some of them eventually move back, if their incomes permit it. Washington still has crime problems and other big-city ills, but I am optimistic about the long-range picture for the District of Columbia.

A team of urban designers, city officials, and academicians who toured European cities to determine how they kept their "ambience, vitality, and excitement" found more than four hundred German cities that had set aside areas for pedestrians where automobile traffic is prohibited.[3] Bicycles are encouraged in a variety of ways, with Bremen even providing specially painted bicycles for citizens to borrow free and drop off at any other bicycle station. They found cities that operate their transit systems on the honor system: no attendant or machine checks to see if a rider has paid. They found much greater emphasis on the arts and their importance to the survival and life of the city than in the United States, a matter of no small importance (see Chapter Nine).

The emphasis on nonautomotive transportation in Europe and Japan needs to be encouraged in our cities. Despite rosy initial forecasts, when mass-transit systems are built or renovated, they do not make money or even come close to breaking even. But the Metro in the District of Columbia, for example, is a tremendous asset to the greater Washington area; it pays for itself in less air pollution and more tourists who can be accommodated. If it is important to the nation that the cities become more livable, then the national budget should reflect greater concern for the costs of mass-transit systems. Some combination of assistance for the badly dilapidated rural bridges and urban mass transit makes political and practical sense. Several mass-transit systems are near bankruptcy. Birmingham, Alabama, closed down its entire bus system for three months during the winter of 1981 for lack of funds. New York City's system is gradually disintegrating with 71,773 breakdowns in 1980 compared to 43,683 in 1979. Separate lanes and streets for buses are being tried in some cities. And why this nation does not provide more bicycle paths — *real* ones, not just roads marked with bicycle signs — both in our cities and across the nation I do not understand. Oregon is the only state to do this in a substantial way. Everytime a new highway or road is built we ought to devote 1 percent of the total appropriation to a parallel bicycle path. We ought to require this at least in all new subdivision developments.

Crime is not particularly different in kind in the cities from what it is elsewhere, but it is intensified and spreads more quickly in the cities. Young people living in rural areas have more options, and when in a rural or suburban area crime does occur, it rarely becomes a catalyst for a large number of others. But because the crime rate is higher in urban areas, anything that reduces crime nationally will help cities. Chief Justice Warren Burger has sensibly recommended that prisons should be used to teach basic literacy and marketable skills, and that the FBI should have a school for prison guards, just as there is one for local police. His suggestions are not likely to be followed, for no state legislator, no congressman, makes votes back home by improving prisons. Yet most of those now in prison will soon be walking the streets, perhaps more prone to crime after the prison experience. It is still true in most prisons that, if you enter without the ability to read and write, you leave the same way; if you go in without a marketable skill, you come out without one. But there are other things besides prison reform that can help.

The courts must move swiftly on those charged with crimes, something they rarely do. A sure, swift sentence deters crime; endless delays encourage people to believe they can get away with criminal activity. Once a person is convicted of a crime of violence (including burglary), the sentence should be promptly imposed and should begin. If an appeal is made, the offender should serve in prison while under appeal. In addition to other benefits from such a change, it would eliminate the ridiculous situation where someone is found guilty of a burglary or a murder, goes out on appeal and commits the same crime while on appeal — sometimes to pay for his lawyer's services.

Improvement of foster-home situations, as well as institutional settings, is important. Eleven-year-old Hector was removed from his home in New York City because of child abuse. He spent the remaining ten years of his life in twenty-eight different institutions at a cost of over $250,000. He committed suicide.[4] One girl who had been in seventeen different foster homes told me that she had never been in a home where anyone cared for her. Churches and synagogues and other volunteers can be of help in securing good foster homes, in providing "Big Brothers" or "Big Sisters" to boys and girls who find themselves in trouble.

One company in New York City has "adopted" a four-block area of the city, using its resources and volunteer personnel to help an impoverished area. In Cincinnati, executives of Procter and Gamble and Taft Broadcasting have volunteered to help in practical ways in an inner-city area, learning the problems of poverty in Cincinnati in the process. A men's organization of a church once contacted me to say it wanted to do something of a civic nature to help the community. The day before, an ex-convict from the same city had happened to stop by my office, desperately seeking a job. I suggested to the men's club that a great project would be to find a job for this man, who did not want to go back to a life of crime. They had a lengthy discussion at their meeting and the president of the club contacted me and asked if I had some other project they could work on. They wanted something a little less controversial. I hasten to add that some church groups are doing an excellent job. The federal volunteer program VISTA gives people in cities a chance to help themselves. California has a California Conservation Corps, using eighteen hundred volunteers, many from the inner cities. Other states and cities could do the same. A literacy corps of volunteers might be formed to work with the tens of thousands in every city (and in rural areas) who cannot read and write. It would be a great experience for both the volunteer and the person who learns these basic skills.

Cities in Europe and other areas have one great advantage over the United States: their populations are less mobile. We do almost nothing to encourage people to spend a lifetime in one place. We view our easy mobility as a great national virtue, and it has advantages. But it also has disadvantages. Some students of the American scene believe that one of the reasons for our high crime rate compared to almost all countries is that we do not establish roots. One out of five Americans moves every year. We do not feel an obligation to those around us, a sense of community identification that is both a help on personal problems and a restraint on conduct. If people viewed the city, not as a place to escape from, but a place to live in, throwing a beer bottle on the sidewalk would be less acceptable behavior. And how can an urban school really educate when there sometimes is a turnover of more than 50 percent in the classroom in one year, in the very neighborhoods that most desperately need every educational advantage? The problem is not solely an urban problem; it is everywhere. We should study the possibility of changing our tax laws so that an additional $100 per person tax deduction is available when the person and his dependents have lived in the same location five or more years, limiting this to no more than four deductions per return, so that we do not encourage population growth. Those who do not pay taxes would be entitled to a payment of $100 per person, a maximum of $400 per household. If such a plan would stabilize neighborhoods and discourage excessive movement, it would be a dividend-paying investment in a better tomorrow for the entire nation, particularly for urban areas. To those who say the poor will suffer under such a program, the reality is that the poor would be among the major beneficiaries if the plan worked, for they are the ones who suffer poor-quality educational opportunities; and they are the ones who primarily suffer from the crime that grows in part out of rootlessness.

The most creative federal program for the cities is the Urban Development Action Grant (UDAG). It requires private investment at a minimum of six dollars for each federal dollar and most programs result in a substantially greater than six-to-one ratio. Although it is designed for urban areas, it can also be used in rural areas of great economic need. The great advantage of the program is that it is not a one-time grant that fixes a street or sewer system and offers temporary employment, but it represents long-term private investment and employment in an area of great need. Areas that have used the program uniformly praise it. UDAG should be expanded.

The simple question of adequate revenue to run cities means that revenue sharing is not a desirable luxury, but a necessity for the operation of this nation's urban centers. Reagan administration attempts to cut back on revenue sharing, whatever that program's flaws in original concept, is an attack on the ability of the cities to sustain themselves.

Finally, every city is unique and ought to build on that uniqueness to attract industries and people into the city and to add to the quality of life, as planner James Rouse has done in Baltimore. In all cities there are programs that are not unique, that can be copied by other cities. Toronto, for example, now requires that all new office buildings include some apartments, so that the city does not become a lifeless beast at night. Other cities should do the same. For a city to build and revive itself, there must be a healthy mix of creativity and practicality. James Rouse has said it well: "We have lived so long with grim, congested, worn-out inner cities and sprawling, cluttered outer cities, that we have subconsciously come to accept them as inevitable and unavoidable. Deep down in our national heart is a lack of conviction that cities can be beautiful, humane, and truly responsive to the needs and yearnings of our people."[5]

In the nineteenth century one of the thrusts of the nation was westward expansion. When Franklin D. Roosevelt became president he focused on the South and its economic problems, significant by any measure. There are those who now say the next fiscal and programmatic thrust must be back to the Northeast and Midwest and they cite statistics to justify that. Since Illinois is one of those states, I have a built-in sympathy for that suggestion, but I do not believe that either Congress or the American public is going to develop any great sympathy for such states as Illinois, New York, and Ohio. There is a recognition that we are states with massive resources. But I believe that sensible attention can be focused on a great challenge to the nation: making our cities more livable. Sound programs can receive both congressional and public support, and not simply from people who live in the cities.

This nation's cities can be beautiful; they can be good and safe places to live, with schools of excellence; cities can contribute to an improved national quality of life. This will not occur overnight, but it can happen if we want to make it happen.

CHAPTER TWELVE

Energy

The most pressing energy need is a national emergency program. It is incredible that a nation that experienced one Arab embargo, and has some idea of the consequences of that, could still not have an emergency program in place a decade later. If there is one word that clearly describes the Middle East it is *unstable,* and that instability could erupt at any point in consequences similar to, or much worse than, the original Arab oil boycott.

Economic boycotts of any variety do not tend to have a long-term impact, but a short-term major dislocation problem could occur in the United States if an Arab boycott were to be combined with a Soviet cutoff to Western Europe. From there any number of scenarios can be put together. What would Nigeria do, for example? Nigeria is now one of our major oil suppliers; it has some ties with the other members of the Organization of Petroleum Exporting Countries (OPEC) and the United States, but strongly opposes the Reagan administration's cozying up to South Africa. Would Nigeria use such circumstances to push a changed U.S. policy on South Africa?

The greater likelihood of danger today is some form of warfare or terrorism, rather than boycott, cutting off oil supplies, hurting us significantly, and devastating Western Europe and Japan. A few years ago I visited the oil fields of Saudi Arabia and what impressed me most was not the technology, or the miles of pipe, but the extreme vulnerability of these resources to even the most primitive forms of attack or sabotage.

A country as security conscious as the United States generally maintains an amazingly indifferent attitude toward what clearly is the major security threat we now face. Some type of dislocation in the Middle East is hundreds of times more likely to occur than a Soviet invasion of Western Europe, yet we devote tens of billions of dollars to the one threat and almost totally ignore the other. We are gradually — much too slowly — filling our strategic petroleum reserve, but that is hardly a substitute for a ready-and-waiting policy to deal with an emergency. We are spending eight times as much on military research as we are on energy research.

It is not only the security of the United States that is threatened by our inattention to the energy problem. The less we plan for an emergency and the more dependent we are on the Middle East for oil, the greater the likelihood that when an emergency does occur we will resort to force to "solve" the problem. With the world teetering on the edge of a nuclear abyss, the United States is twiddling its thumbs rather than moving to an emergency plan or plans, rather than promoting real conservation, rather than promoting use of coal instead of oil — and so on, *ad infinitum*. Nowhere is an accidental confrontation with the Soviets more likely to occur than in the Middle East. Nowhere are troop movements and display of weaponry less likely to be effective — even counterproductive — than in the Middle East. Instead of developing an energy policy, we send an aircraft carrier and accompanying flotilla to that region in the belief that we are doing something. Whatever stability our military presence renders is more than offset by the instability of our lack of an energy policy.

While the energy cloud grows darker and darker, the Reagan administration takes these stands:

1. Proposes eliminating the Department of Energy.
2. Wants a cutback in the budget for data collection on energy, reducing our already limited ability to know where we stand and where we soon will be.
3. Rejects congressional efforts to provide clear legal authority to allocate energy resources where needed in the event of a serious shortage.
4. Rejects all plans to restrict uses of energy.

Not only must we formulate a policy for an emergency, but we also need a substantial development of what now can be called an energy policy by only the loosest definition. The price of oil has been deregulated; beyond that we have done little. Deregulation has resulted in increased exploration for oil, but the United States is likely to continue its production decline and by the end of the century almost all experts agree that world production of oil will be descending. Federal officials predict a decline in U.S. production of at least one million barrels a day by the end of this decade. And we are in the uncomfortable position of having almost half of our energy consumption dependent on oil.

Efforts to formulate a policy have been retarded by the resistance of some to even having a policy. The November 1981 *Harper's* has a front-page declaration: "The Energy Crisis is Over." David Stockman, head of the Office of Management and Budget, wrote an article while serving in the House that attacked the idea of having an energy policy. In 1978 he described the oil crisis as "largely a media event" and asserted: "The global economic conditions necessary for another major unilateral price action by OPEC are not likely to emerge for more than a decade — if ever."[1] Pleased that no energy program was adopted, Stockman said the political system had escaped "momentary energy jingoism. We have declined to launch what would have become a disastrous, inextricable engagement in an unnecessary war." He said that the unduly pessimistic calls for an energy policy on the basis of further OPEC price rises were like Chicken Little's claim that the sky was falling. Within one year of the appearance of Stockman's article, world oil prices more than doubled. Those of us who write have the problem of being outrageously wrong on occasion. (My friend Milton Friedman did even worse. In March 1974 he predicted that oil prices were about to drop to "a dime a barrel.")[2] Despite all that had happened, the industrialized West increased oil consumption 7.4 percent between January 1978 and January 1979. Since that time both consumption and importation of oil have tapered off.

The United States must have an energy policy to deal with an emergency and policies that encourage conservation; it must encourage international as well as domestic competition; it must promote coal research and development; it must sensibly approach the synthetic-fuel potential; it must encourage solar energy; it must push nuclear *fusion* research; and it must work with the OPEC countries on their long-range economic problems. Our record in these areas is not good.

The rise in the price of oil has done more to encourage conservation than anything else. In 1940 oil sold on the world market for $0.75 a barrel. In 1970 it sold for $1.80. On January 1, 1975, Arab light sold for $10.46 a barrel. And now prices range from $30 to $40 a barrel. Prices quadrupled in 1974 and then doubled in 1979. The cost of jet fuel has jumped 900 percent in the last decade. At fifty-two, I am old enough to remember gasoline selling for less than twenty cents a gallon. The price of natural gas is going up; bottled-gas prices have skyrocketed; coal and even wood costs have risen much faster than the rate of inflation. The price changes have caused more homes to be insulated, new homes to be built with a southern exposure, people to drive less, and even car manufacturers to produce cars that give much more mileage per gallon. Corporations are making significant energy reductions; AT&T expects its 1984 business to double that for 1973 and use less energy than in 1973. Union Carbide, one of the largest industrial users in the nation, had expected substantial consumption growth from 1974 through 1990, but has had a year-by-year decline in energy usage.

But millions of homes are without insulation. A substantial percentage of the nation's population still believes there is no energy problem and are convinced the entire matter has been created by a few large oil companies, perhaps with the help of government; they see no need (other than price) to try to conserve. There has been a gradual educational process taking place, but millions of Americans do not understand the small steps each of us can take to save energy.

Although conservation lacks the drama of new programs and is wrongly labeled by some as a no-growth policy for the economy, if we had seriously attacked the conservation issue when we first knew of oil problems, it is unlikely that we would have anywhere near the present prices. Much to the consternation of our friends in Western Europe and Japan, and to the annoyance of those OPEC nations sympathetic to us, such as Saudi Arabia, we talked about doing things but did almost nothing. Between 1973 and 1978 our consumption of oil did not decline, but rose by 1.5 million barrels per day. As one study notes: "The Administration, for the most part either opposed or gave only weak, distracted support to the conservation initiative."[3] And another writer observes accurately: "The real problem is uncertain presidential and congressional leadership interested more in not upsetting the voters rather than in developing a coherent energy policy."[4] The commission appointed by President Carter to look at where the nation should go in the next decade reported on one of his last days in office: "Conservation represents the cheapest, quickest, surest, and least risky way to limit U.S. reliance on imported oil."[5]

One action that would help the nation in every way would be to mandate an energy audit on all homes and require that all homes be insulated within seven years. Thirty percent of the homes in the nation have no insulation, not even storm doors and windows. Utilities can finance, and in many cases are financing, insulation, paid for by a small monthly amount on utility bills, usually more than compensating for the savings in heat or air conditioning.

There are poor and elderly whose incomes are so low that they are forced by circumstances to be so frugal that they use little heat and no air conditioning. In those cases some type of VISTA or CETA program ought to combine this need with the resources of the unemployed to see that those homes are insulated. This is important because theoretical "solutions" to the energy problem too easily fall upon the poor. Economist Lester Thurow has pointed out: "While a 100 percent increase in the price of energy would reduce the real income of the average American by 9.9 percent, it would reduce the real income of the poorest decile of families by 34 percent and the richest decile by five percent."[6] If a program were inaugurated to make sure every home in the nation is insulated within seven years, everyone would benefit. It would save more than five hundred thousand barrels of oil a day. The difficulty is that there are few lobbyists for this type of effort, with the possible exception of the insulation manufacturers, whom I have not seen on the Washington scene. Conservation is a worthy cause without much support.

Industries and municipalities must be encouraged to imaginatively convert their liabilities into assets. Energy from garbage is one example; fertilizer from sewage is another. Sweden, the Netherlands, and Denmark convert more than 40 percent of their municipal garbage into energy, while in the United States less than one percent is converted. A federal study shows that without great efforts we could increase the conversion to 18 percent, saving 132,000 barrels of oil a day. The paper industry, faced with environmental problems from sulfur, has converted that liability into a money-maker. The automobile industry complained about mileage figures imposed on them by government — but those governmental leaders and environmentalists who were so roundly denounced may have saved two of the major automobile companies from their own folly and destruction. Even with those imposed mileage figures, and all of the gasoline they saved, Chrysler still is in a nip-and-tuck battle for survival.

Los Angeles's source of electricity is oil, and after the oil embargo of 1973 that city faced a real crunch. A blue-ribbon committee set mandatory targets for all customers; users had to reduce consumption by 12 percent over the previous year, or face a 50-percent increase in their utility bill. The result was an 18-percent drop in consumption, and even after the Arabs lifted the embargo and the penalty had been dropped electric consumption remained below the 1973 levels. The people and businesses of Los Angeles had learned to live comfortably with less electricity.

There are hundreds of good energy-saving devices hidden away in the garages and basements of this nation. I have probably thirty people in my district with patents on some type of energy-saving device, but the nation discourages them rather than encourages them. Perhaps twenty-eight of the thirty patents are not worth anything. But if two are useful and if the same is true in each of the other 434 congressional districts, approximately 900 devices that could save an appreciable amount of energy are almost literally buried in this country. Don Smith has one of these. It saves heat that now goes up a chimney. It has met all the safety tests by the various agencies. He approached the utilities that sell gas, thinking that they would be interested since he had read their advertisements on how they were trying to save energy. He found that these companies, which profess great interest in conservation, not only were disinterested, but downright hostile. He is now going to larger businesses, getting them to agree to use his device if he gets a percentage of the savings. He is not getting rich, but he is making a living *and saving the nation energy.* If his device is as good as it appears to be, hundreds of thousands of homes and offices should be installing it instead of a handful. Are none of the ideas people have for gas-saving devices on cars any good? My reluctant conclusion is that we have made it too difficult and complicated to patent something, and then it is too easy for the industry it affects to smother the result. Perhaps none of the energy-saving devices in the garages and basements of America will produce dramatic results, but there are ideas out there that ought to see the light of day, ideas that could save a significant amount of energy. One of the problems with our economic corporate concentration is that it becomes more difficult for ideas to emerge. The nation still has Thomas Edisons, but we put senseless obstacles in their way.

Other ideas will *not* emerge from the basements and garages of the country and will take a substantial federal investment. For example, ocean tides go in and out at certain precise, known times and contain tremendous power. But except for two limited experiments, the nation has not seriously looked at creating hydroelectric power from the ocean tides. Some day it will happen. Geothermal energy is being pursued more aggressively and also has potential. Gasohol is expensive but is more than a theory and can be produced from a variety of substances, everything from just plain garbage to sawdust to sugar to cornstalks and crude oil byproducts. Depending on whose figures are used, somewhere around 1.4 million barrels of oil equivalent are now being saved annually because of gasohol, not a huge figure for a nation that imports several times that amount every day, but a substantial figure when you realize that the federal government has done more discouraging than encouraging. A word of caution on gasohol, however: it can be produced from cornstalks and other field growth without using corn and wheat or the grains themselves. The food products can be used, however, and it would be both politically imprudent and wrong from a humanitarian viewpoint to eventually devote a sizable portion of our grain production to fuel our luxury cars, rather than getting food to the desperately hungry. Such an eventuality should be carefully avoided.

One of the ways we can marginally help keep international oil prices down, and at the same time foster domestic competition, is to do what many nations do: have a quasi-government corporation that buys all the oil from abroad. If Texaco or Mobil or anyone else wants one million barrels of light crude in ninety days, the bid forms go out and the country with the lowest bid gets the business. Our nation believes in competition and the benefits of the free-enterprise system generally, but we have failed to apply competition as much as we should to oil. The experience of other nations is that bidding does bring the price down slightly — not by any huge numbers — and of equal importance, it is easier for the small refiner to participate on an equal basis with the major ones.

If such a corporation charged a 1-percent fee for its services, it could be self-financing and the substantial balance could be used to match, perhaps on a one-to-four basis, investments by American oil companies in exploration in the developing nations. There are many nations where there has been only minimal exploration for oil and natural gas. The more we can diversify our sources of imported oil, the less harm interruptions of supply are likely to cause. From 1969 to 1973, 92 percent of the increase in the world's oil production came from the Persian Gulf. That number has since been somewhat reduced, but less reliance on one volatile area for oil is clearly in the national interest. That takes on added importance when one recognizes that the Soviet Union is the world's largest oil-producing country. Almost half of Soviet hard-currency earnings come from oil sales. Soviet exports to other countries will gradually decline as more and more is consumed domestically. Since we are dealing with a world market, the more that can be produced, whatever the source, the more likely we are to avoid price escalations of an extravagant nature, the more sure our supply will be beyond the end of this century, and the developing nation that is helped can become a better trading partner with the United States for our other products.

I do not join those who want to close the existing nuclear power plants. Much more important than the Three Mile Island type of potential accident is the whole question of nuclear waste. I don't want it in my district and I know of no member of Congress who does. Talk of taking it to some foreign country is international idiocy. Two facts are clear: first, it is not likely that new nuclear plants will be started in the next decade; second, even if they are, they will serve utilities that are largely coal operations anyway, and they will do little to reduce our dependence on foreign oil. Not unimportant is the reality that nuclear energy costs far more than once was estimated.

One of the products we ought to be promoting much more vigorously is coal. Estimates vary widely on how much coal we have, but it is enough to handle *all* of our energy needs for several centuries. Our coal use is increasing slightly. Coal is here in abundance; it is reliable; and it is less expensive than oil. Using coal is anti-inflationary. Unfortunately, coal is not exotic, and spending money on coal research seems to have little appeal to those in charge of energy for the federal government. The last major innovation in the underground mines, the continuous miner, came into use more than twenty years ago. After President Carter made a speech in which he lauded coal as an energy resource, the Associated Press called me and I told them I hoped the Secretary of Energy, James Schlesinger, listened because I had not detected the same priorities in the Energy Department that I heard in the president's speech. The first Reagan budget follows the familiar pattern: less money on coal research, more money on nuclear research. The only major coal-research laboratory in the heart of the bituminous coal states has been closed. If this nation had spent one-tenth as much on coal research in the last thirty years as we have spent on nuclear-fission research, the nation would not be in its present awkward energy position. And we would have better answers for pollution control for coal, a problem that troubles our neighbors in Canada particularly. The Ontario Ministry of the Environment claims one hundred lakes have been "killed" by acid rain; Norway and Sweden have the same complaints about their European neighbors to the south. More and better research could test the validity of these claims.

Greater conventional use of coal should be encouraged rather than discouraged, and research should move forward much more aggressively on improving present methods of making coal use safe for our air. The technology now exists in coal-cleaning devices, scrubbers, and fluidized beds to use high-sulfur coal and meet any existing air-effluent standards. Georgetown University in the heart of Washington, D.C., for example, uses a fluidized bed and high-sulfur coal and I have never read or heard a complaint about it. Perhaps the most successful scrubber operator is the utility for the City of Louisville, a reality some utilities don't want to acknowledge.

State regulatory agencies in the Midwest and East are discouraging the use of coal and costing consumers and the nation a great deal in the process. Utilities can now automatically pass through increases in the costs of fuel — including transportation — to their users. So utilities in Illinois and other states that use Montana and Colorado and Utah coal, which has a low sulfur content but also a low heat capacity, pay $18 to $40 a ton for railroad costs. This is automatically added to the utility bills of consumers. If those same utilities want to have a fluidized bed (which generally can be done only on a new plant) or a scrubber to clean the Illinois coal, the utilities have to go through lengthy hearings to get the approval of the regulatory agency to pay for a capital improvement. The losers are the consumers, who pay higher bills; Illinois and Indiana and Ohio coal miners, who are not working; and the nation, for a huge amount of oil is consumed each day by railroad trains hauling coal from the western states to Illinois.

We should also be doing much more to promote exports of coal, both because it helps our balance of trade and because it means that the recipient countries are less reliant on the instabilities inherent in the OPEC situation. Export demand is rising rapidly. In 1980 coal-export orders increased 42.5 percent over 1979, and when the final figures are computed for 1981 and 1982, significant growth is expected in both years. But exporting coal requires adequate rail and port facilities, both of which we are neglecting.

Coal can also be used for synthetic production of "natural" gas and for producing a high-quality oil. Precisely what our status is on natural gas is a matter of considerable dispute, but the conclusion of one study appears to be reasonable: that it will be a challenge "to find enough new gas reserves to maintain production at current levels."[7] We are in a better position than the dire forecasts of a few years ago would have had us believe, but not in good shape. We need synthetic production. President Carter asked for $88 billion for synthetic-fuel development, an astronomical sum. Congress, acting with some prudence, has provided $17 billion, and the Reagan administration seems to be moving most reluctantly toward that. Synthetic fuels are not the panacea some profess them to be, but it is ironic that South Africa is completing its third major coal-gasification and liquifaction plant at a cost of more than $3 billion, while the United States, with the world's largest coal reserves, has yet to complete its first major coal-gasification or liquifaction plant. The Reagan administration position is that this is an area the private sector should handle. It is hard to argue with that theory, but the practical reality is that any commercial synthetic-fuels plant will cost more than $1 billion. Unless there is a government price guarantee of some variety, the investor stands to lose the entire amount if OPEC, for example, would suddenly and significantly drop the price of oil. No one believes they will do that, but if your billion dollars were at stake, you would be unwilling to make the venture. (It reportedly costs Saudi Arabia forty cents to produce a barrel of oil.) Some type of government involvement is essential if the nation is to move ahead on synthetic fuels. But even if we move ahead — and we should — this source will not provide substantial alternatives to oil until well into the next decade. The weakness of synthetic-fuel plans is that they are based on present technology, using western low-sulfur coal. That poses a problem because, whether liquifaction or gasification is the end product, synthetic fuels require a great amount of water, and the West is already short of water. The Midwest has water in abundance, but has high-sulfur coal. The Reagan administration is unwilling to spend money on research for utilization of high-sulfur coal.

One observation on coal development and utilization I cannot prove but I believe to be true is that the increasing control of the major oil companies over coal production and reserves is discouraging the development of coal. When the price of gasoline goes up one cent, that brings in more than $1 billion of revenue. Faced with the choice of promoting coal research and development, and thereby decreasing demand and price on oil products, or continuing the status quo on coal and seeing oil prices rise, it is understandable that coal does not receive a high priority. The Knight-Ridder newspapers assigned two Pulitzer Prize–winning reporters, Donald Barlett and James Steele, to a one-year study of energy. They reached the same conclusion.

Following the death of Archbishop Makarios, the first president of Cyprus, President Carter appointed a United States delegation to attend the funeral services and tributes and I was among those appointed. While in Nicosia, Cyprus, one of the other members, Senator Charles Mathias, a Republican from Maryland, and I decided to visit refugee housing. We discovered that each of these refugee houses — for which 55 percent of the building costs were covered by U.S. funds — had a solar-heating unit for hot water. We can spend our money for solar heating units in Cyprus, but we do not spend money for them in Carbondale, Illinois, or Storm Lake, Iowa, or Cottage Grove, Oregon, or Bangor, Maine, or anywhere else in the United States. I do not fault the Cypriots; they are using common sense. In the United States, 14 to 25 percent of the energy used in a home goes for hot-water heat, and it is probably a higher percentage in Cyprus. But if they can exercise such common sense in Cyprus, why can't we do it here?

Most statistics I read suggest that solar energy can supply only a small percentage of energy by the end of the century, some say less than 1 percent. The editor of *World Oil* says that over the next twenty-five years solar energy will have the impact of "a mosquito bite on an elephant's fanny."[8] The organizer of International Sun Day says it will supply 40 percent.[9] Most estimates are on the low side. But that assumes we proceed at the present pace — if you can call it that — toward greater solar utilization. That assumes that both Congress and the president continue to treat solar energy as if it were a relative with venereal disease: we acknowledge its existence but we don't get too close. Solar energy is still in a fairly primitive state, but it will not be perfected and improved unless and until we encourage greater use, and that will only come through federal leadership. That means more tax incentives. Why not solar hot-water heating units on public housing here, if we can pay for them in Nicosia? Should new federal buildings use oil and gas when we presumably want to shift away from those sources? We have a new federal building in Carbondale, Illinois, with solar heating. The General Services Administration of the federal government was — and is — not enthusiastic about the idea, but how can the U.S. government tell General Motors and others to try solar energy if the federal government is unwilling? The president of the Massachusetts Institute of Technology (MIT) commented recently: "We built the first solar house and we are working on number six now. They are still not economically sensible, although they may be getting closer to being so."[10] With all due respect to MIT, I have seen solar homes that are economically sensible though perhaps not aesthetically attractive. Tens of thousands of American homes now use passive solar heating. We are close to major breakthroughs in solar use, but the public and private sectors must keep pushing. For example, if we can figure some way to give utilities an economic incentive to push solar energy, that would be a major step forward. At present they are less than enthusiastic, for among other things, they see solar energy as no financial help to them and potentially a great liability.

The type of nuclear energy we use today is nuclear *fission* (splitting atoms). A form of energy being sought is nuclear *fusion* (joining atoms) and sometime around the turn of the century, if not before, that probably will become a reality. A former member of the House, Mike McCormack of the state of Washington, is a nuclear physicist and he says that the breakthrough on nuclear fusion will be the most important energy development since the discovery of fire. Proponents say it is clean, inexpensive (renewing itself), with no weapons-reprocessing potential and no environmental hazards.

Princeton University now leads the nation in this expensive research, but we tend to blow hot and cold in our efforts. It is years enough away that no one in Congress and no president will receive credit for pushing it. And delay causes no political problems. Few people in any congressional district have even heard about nuclear fusion. But research on this should receive a high priority for the nation.

An energy problem of worldwide dimensions that indirectly affects the United States is the shortage of wood, still the world's number-one fuel. The majority of the world's population relies on wood for almost all its energy-related needs. Growing populations have caused stripped forests. Indirectly, this has an impact on U.S. energy problems, for as wood disappears, people must move to other energy sources, including oil. The renewal of wood resources is essential for the world's poor, but in a decision less publicized than the Reagan administration's incredibly insensitive go-it-alone on infant formula (119 to 1 vote in the World Health Organization), which established a code of ethics for companies that promote infant-milk formula rather than breast-feeding, the Reagan administration forced the World Bank to hold off on a program to prepare for planting more trees in the developing nations, apparently to avoid agreeing to pay our share for such a program. Again, our position was one of lonely eminence. A meeting in Nairobi was prepared to launch a five-year program, but the Reagan administration felt it was not in our national interest to cooperate. The plans remain dormant.

Finally, let us acknowledge that we will continue to import oil and let us work with the oil-producing countries on some of their long-range plans. In visiting Saudi Arabia a few years ago I noted the tremendous amount of construction under way, and a Saudi official, pointing to a building crane, said with a smile: "That's our national bird." The Saudis are moving ahead, but there are great uncertainties in their future. People in Saudi Arabia and Kuwait and other countries from which we purchase oil should feel that they are not simply being used. They should sense a genuine concern on the part of our officials about the long-range picture for these countries. They should be asking themselves: What happens when the oil is gone? We should share in both asking the question and assisting in finding answers. We cannot agree with them on everything in world affairs, the Israeli question clearly being an irritant, but though they do not endorse our close ties to Israel (and we should not back off on this), they will be pleased to work with us if they find us looking at them as friends, not just oil suppliers. We convey the right attitude — and the wrong attitude — in a thousand small ways, and too often now we are conveying the wrong attitude, even with television shows that rarely show good Arabs. If they sense genuine friendship on our part, boycotts or embargoes are unlikely and terrorism less likely. If they sense hostility, aloofness, indifference, or arrogance, then they will not go out of their way to accommodate us. Our exchange must be more than dollars for oil.

In 1973, with much fanfare, Project Independence was announced by President Nixon. At that time the United States imported approximately 6 million barrels of oil a day. Four years later that had reached 8.6 million barrels a day.

In April 1977 President Carter announced his first energy program and called it the "moral equivalent of war," unfortunately dubbed MEOW by less-than-respectful legislators and reporters. Project Independence was doomed, and we have not had anything close to the "moral equivalent of war." In the last year of the Carter administration progress in conservation became a reality — not a dramatic reality, but an indication that our energy patterns can change. Our goals should be realistic. The problem is a real one and it must be addressed firmly. We have pontificated long enough. Speeches must be replaced by action.

CHAPTER THIRTEEN

Defense

T here is no dispute in the United States on the need for adequate defense. But there can be and should be considerable discussion about what is meant by "adequate" and how that is best attained. And what is a good defense should not be so "good" that it erodes the economic base of the country. Most of the oratory on this issue is like snow — it is beautiful as it descends from above, but when you hold it in your hand to examine, its substance disappears.

"I just can't discuss defense spending rationally in my district," one of my colleagues told me recently. Since he feels he can't discuss it rationally — and since I assume he has to discuss it — my conclusion is that he discusses it irrationally. Although I have not heard his discussions of defense spending and priorities, I have heard so much irrational speech making on this issue that I could probably give his speech for him. Which candidate advocates spending more on defense is not the test of who is the greater patriot when choosing between candidates. If there is one area of national spending, above all others, in which we should use our head rather than our heart, it is in the security of this nation. If the race between the two political parties is to see who can spend more on defense, then national security will be the loser. Democrats ought to be structuring a meaningful dialogue by talking sense. In some places around the country Republican counterparts will respond and do the same, and the nation can emerge the winner.

Let me outline in question-and-answer form what I believe are the basics of where we now stand.

What is the fundamental flaw in our approach to national defense spending and authorizations?

When we talk about "defense" and "security," we think solely in terms of weapons systems and management. Our security interests are much broader. Oil is a practical illustration. For us to have the finest of weapons but no emergency plan for handling a cutoff of oil from the Middle East is preposterous. Or consider another illustration. About one-fourth of our defense budget is geared to the possibility that the Soviets may send tanks into Central Europe. The chance of that happening is a fraction of 1 percent. One military leader is quoted as saying it is one chance out of fifty thousand, though no one can measure that unlikely event precisely. Whatever the likelihood, we cannot ignore the possibility. But the chance that the Soviets will try to take advantage of hunger and chaos and misery in one of the developing nations is ninety-nine out of a hundred. Yet the Reagan administration and the Congress — including a large number of Democrats — are willing to sign a blank check on the Central European remote possibility, but want to cut back dramatically on foreign economic assistance to countries where we *know* the Soviets will try to take advantage of a problem. Is that rational? We spend, by way of comparison, twice as much to train our military personnel as all of South Asia spends for the education of their 300 million school-age children. We have to make better judgments about where our spending will provide greater security.

As another example, nothing we could do would strengthen our security more than to put our economic house in order, for we are roughly one-third of the world's economy. If we get our economy in better shape, then many other nations tied to our economy in myriad ways will have a better chance to put themselves in a stronger economic position. There are even some who believe that the great long-range danger to the United States and the Soviet Union is not that we will destroy each other physically with nuclear weapons, but that we will destroy each other economically through the perceived necessity of stockpiling nuclear weapons and their delivery systems. If we have a stronger economy, we provide an example and an attraction for the developing nations, many of whom are deciding between a Marxist system, our system, or a mixture that meshes with their particular needs. As President Dwight D. Eisenhower noted shortly after he retired from the presidency: "If we put one more dollar in a weapons system than we should, we are weakening the defense of the United States."[1] But the nation does not even view the economic picture as part of the security problem — even though many top military personnel of this nation do.

The United States must move away from a myopic view of security.

Do we have weapons-related needs?

Yes, we do, but they are not the needs that generally show up on charts and graphs. Our greatest needs are in conventional forces, particularly in manpower, operations, and maintenance. We don't have enough spare parts, for example. We have planes that can't fly because of lack of small spare parts, tanks that can't move, mortars that can't be fired, and the list continues. Meeting this kind of practical need has no political mileage. And no one is pushing for it. I have yet to meet the person who walks up to me and says, "I'm the lobbyist for spare parts."

We also need simpler, less complicated, often lighter weapons. We "test" equipment under ideal circumstances too often, not in deserts or rain or the circumstances under which it may be used. And the more complicated weapons become, the more difficult it is to get personnel to operate them and the more likely they are to break down; a weapon with one thousand parts is more likely to break down than a weapon with one hundred. We need practical, *usable* equipment. Our Black Hawk helicopter has 257 knobs and switches, 135 circuit breakers, 62 displays, and an instrument and control panel that covers 11.7 square feet. We also need smaller equipment. Our large, new tank is good in theory, but it takes our largest cargo plane (of which we have seventy-seven) to haul one tank. Does it make sense to build five thousand of these huge, complicated tanks?

A new nuclear carrier today will cost about $4 billion, and the fleet of ships that must accompany a carrier for protection doubles that cost. Cruise missiles and smaller ships make a great deal more sense as the navy grows. But even when both the president and Joint Chiefs of Staff say we need no more large carriers, the pressure from all those emotionally involved — or those making carriers — is great enough so that Congress votes another carrier anyway. Part of the pressure comes from admirals who whisper to members of Congress that we really do need another supercarrier, despite what their boss is saying.

And many members of Congress fail to note one simple reality: no sea captain prefers to be in charge of a small ship.

When we neglect conventional forces and pile our money into bigger and fancier weapons systems, then we limit our response possibilities. If the Soviets move their tanks somewhere, we ought to have an alternative other than blowing up civilization with nuclear warheads. Our great need is not more and bigger and better strategic weaponry, but the ability to deal more effectively with situations that call for a limited, more relative response.

Are the West European nations going to join us in large defense-expenditure increases?

No. There will be some increases, some decreases, but nowhere near our effort. No European nation devotes as high a percentage of its gross national product to defense as we do, although several now have higher per-capita incomes. A top French defense expert put it accurately: "Given the economic, social and domestic political constraints at work in most European countries, a drastic increase of European defense budgets seems unrealistic."[2] Incredibly, we are now preparing for World War III by pulling out of mothballs almost antique battleships, easy targets for any missile, while the British Royal Navy is retiring one-third of its largest ships. Japan spends about one-sixth as much as we do on defense on a per-capita basis. The United States is alone among the Western powers in launching a massive arms buildup.

Are we behind the Soviets militarily at this point?

No, although in many respects the gap between our two nations is closing. And there are areas where the Soviets are ahead. In chemical warfare, for example. In numbers of submarines they are also ahead of us, though our smaller numbers are much quieter and on balance we still maintain solid superiority in this field. We have about half again as many strategic nuclear warheads. The Soviets have more tanks, but we have much better antitank weapons. A tank is an effective weapon against a civilian population, but some believe it is almost as outmoded as the cavalry against a militarily sophisticated opponent. The tanks represent a threat to the Communist nations bordering the Soviet Union, to any developing nation where they might be used, to China — but it is less certain that they represent a significant direct threat to West Germany.

The numbers games become tricky. For example, if you simply make a list of their manpower and compare it to ours in numbers, they are substantially ahead. That has to be modified by the fact that their railroads and defense plants are part of their armed forces, and our Corps of Engineers provides a basically civilian function. Calculating all of that, they are still ahead. But if you add the Warsaw Pact nations and the North Atlantic Treaty Organization (NATO) nations, we are about equal. And where do you fit China into such an equation? The Soviets have about one-fourth of their troops and weaponry along the Chinese border.

I can show you a graph that will indicate the United States is far ahead of the Soviet Union in almost everything — and I can provide another graph that shows the opposite. Both are technically accurate. But the pressure within the United States is to build more and bigger weapons, the cause promoted by those who make money building them (and who believe in their cause, I add in fairness) and by the substantial public-relations machine at the Pentagon.

Full-page advertisements in many of the nation's newspapers in 1980 and 1981 pointed out how many more vessels the Soviet navy has than our navy. A ship manufacturer placed these ads. The ads did not say that, although it is true that they have more vessels, we have half again as much tonnage as they, are far better equipped for operating away from our home base, have much more accurate weapons, have thirteen aircraft carriers to their one. And if our allies are included, our side has more vessels. The ad was accurate as far as it went, but it gave a distorted picture.

If you are talking about the United States versus the Soviet Union, the ultimate question rests in the nuclear-weaponry field. How much nuclear retaliatory response is needed to provide a significant deterrence? For a rational leader over there — or here — even one nuclear bomb ought to be enough of a deterrent. But because that one bomb might not be enough, and because that one bomb might be destroyed, we have made thousands of them. If you move away from the assumption of a rational leader to the possibility of an irrational one (an Idi Amin type), then will even the manufacture and placement of a thousand times as many weapons than we now have be a deterrent?

The military situation comes down to the old question: When is enough, enough? There are no precise answers.

Can we then achieve the "military superiority" the Reagan administration is talking about?
We are ahead, as I have said, but clear-cut superiority, where we can destroy them and they cannot destroy us, is not possible. We fool only ourselves by talking in those terms. It is difficult to measure Soviet expenditures precisely, but the 1979 report of the Arms Control Disarmament Agency of the U.S. government places total NATO and Warsaw Pact expenditures at approximately the same level. What is clear is that, if we spend more, the Soviets will do the same. That is about as rational as a cat chasing its tail.

Why are the Soviets spending so much on defense?
Motivation is always difficult to judge, but some things are clear.
We fear the Soviet Union. No one else.
Militarily, they fear — genuinely fear — the United States, West Germany, and China. And like all dictatorships, their nonmilitary fears include literature that may be brought into the country and matters that their people might learn. One recent visitor to the Soviet Union described that country as "an elephant afraid of mice."[3] They fear us militarily because they do not understand us and our system, and we have enough "nuts" making ridiculous statements that they cannot always distinguish between them and actual government policy. And we respond, or fail to respond, to their overtures in what often appears a surly fashion, because we do not understand them and their system. They fear West Germany in large part for historical reasons. Their country has repeatedly suffered from invasion by the West, and they see West Germany as the only power in Europe that could invade again from the West. The Soviet scars imposed by Germany in the last war are still real. They fear China because of Chinese manpower and potential and because the two nations do not agree on certain portions of their common border.

In addition, the Soviets place no great reliance on their Warsaw Pact colleagues, particularly Poland, Rumania, and Hungary. Someone has said that the Soviet Union is the only nation on the face of the earth surrounded by hostile Communist neighbors. There is a germ of truth to that, though not all of the thirteen nations that border the Soviets are Communist countries.

We are in an infinitely superior strategic position in almost every respect. We are surrounded by two oceans and two friendly neighbors. We have an economy vastly superior to theirs; their gross national product today is probably below Japan's. We are a nation blessed with more natural resources and know-how, particularly the ability to produce food. Our transportation system is far superior. The educational level of our people is higher, though this gap is closing.

But part of the situation can only be described by the word *paranoia*. It is not uncommon in nations that have recently emerged as major powers. They — and we — still feel threatened. They still need to prove to themselves that they are a great power. We fear the power of their competing ideology.

At least some of this Soviet stress on the military is an outgrowth of the Cuban missile crisis. The Soviets don't want to be humiliated again on the international stage.

Do the Soviets want peace?

The best answer to that was given to me by Averill Harriman, who served as ambassador to the Soviet Union from 1943 to 1946 and has had frequent dealings with their leaders since that time. "Perhaps more than any country other than Japan they are peace conscious," he says, "because they have experienced war deeply as we have not. I remember visiting with Brezhnev when he showed me the picture of his first great-grandchild. He had tears in his eyes when he told me he hoped she would never have to go through what he went through. It was not phoney. He meant it. But at the same time the Soviets are interested in promoting their system and sometimes are too adventurous. The danger to the world is that they will misunderstand what we will tolerate, overstep some place and accidentally provoke the holocaust we all want to avoid."

How do we avoid that fatal misunderstanding?

Getting control over miscalculation is not easy.

Theodore Roosevelt's oft-quoted advice to speak softly and carry a big stick in international affairs should be part of the answer. Our political process encourages bellicose statements about the Soviets, just as their system seems to reward bellicose statements about us. Somehow we must mature so that beating the Russians over the head with a verbal two-by-four is not politically rewarding. Less screaming at each other and more conversation would be helpful.

When we say something, however, we should mean it. They respect firmness; they do not like indecision. They want to know where they stand in their relationship with the United States. They also do not like surprises. They are a rather stoic, stable people. Their key personnel illustrate this. Foreign Minister Gromyko has served in that capacity for twenty-four years, a period during which we had eight secretaries of state. Their ambassador to the United States, Anatoly Dobrynin, has been ambassador since 1962; during that period we have had eight ambassadors and two acting ambassadors to the Soviet Union. Before the United States recognized the People's Republic of China, the Soviet's most bitter foe, we did nothing to prepare the USSR. We gave only two hour's advance notice. After the announcement one of our top officials talked about "playing the China card" against the Soviet Union; we needlessly aroused their anger. If we had quietly explained our actions in advance, informing them of what we would soon do, they would not have been pleased, but their response would have been moderated. (Also, we could hardly have treated our old friends in Taiwan more shabbily than we did in the way we handled the matter.) Certain niceties should be learned in domestic or foreign relations: you don't drink beer in the Baptist church basement; you don't ask for a ham sandwich at an Orthodox Jewish fund-raising dinner; and you don't pull surprises on a newly powerful nation that does not like surprises.

Finally, we must be doing a great deal more to promote exchanges and to understand each other, from the grass roots up. We fear what we do not understand; that is true on both sides. That can be said about the United States and *any* other country. Our exchange programs with all countries are shrinking, but in the case of the Soviet Union our lack of understanding is a compounded danger. In fairness it must be added that the Soviets in some ways have made greater efforts toward understanding than we have. There are more teachers of English in the Soviet Union than there are students of Russian in the United States. Recently I visited with Eugene Trani, academic dean of the University of Missouri at Kansas City, who had just completed a semester lecturing in Moscow. What amazed him when he gave a lecture on diplomatic history in English to a class of sixty Soviet graduate students was that all of them understood English well enough to laugh at his jokes. It is particularly unfortunate that we are not making a similar effort to understand their language and system at a time when it has become more open and available. *Washington Post* reporter Robert G. Kaiser notes: "We can follow internal events quite closely; when an important official is promoted or demoted, the reasons are usually not impossible to divine. We know in detail how weak the Soviet economy is, and why. . . . It is still commonplace to describe Russia as a mystery, but in fact the mystery is largely solved."[4] If we do not understand what is happening there, it is, to a great extent, our own fault. In the last three years our already miniscule efforts toward understanding the Russian language have declined as fifty-two colleges and universities have dropped their Russian courses. On top of that, we have only a few in the United States who speak the other languages of the Soviet Union.

I headed the first official congressional delegation to visit the Soviet Union after the Afghanistan invasion. The invasion occurred in December 1979. Our group, three Republican and three Democratic House members, visited the USSR in June 1981. Shortly before we went the State Department refused to renew the U.S. visa of the Soviet's top American specialist, Dr. Georgi Arbatov, who was scheduled to appear on the Bill Moyers television show. And the previous July the Soviets had denied the U.S. ambassador the traditional chance to address the Soviet Union on television on the Fourth of July. At a dinner in Moscow attended by many Soviet officials, I made a toast in which I urged that we take as many small steps toward friendship as possible and avoid the little irritants, such as keeping each other off television. Whether that toast helped or not I do not know, but shortly after that our acting ambassador was able to make his five-minute July Fourth speech to the Soviet Union. I trust we will not keep Soviets off American television again, for both nations learn from these exchanges.

Senator Sam Nunn of Georgia has suggested that United States and Soviet military leaders ought to have a regular exchange — get together, visit in each other's homes, and at least inch forward in this process of understanding. Arms-control specialists should do the same. And all other types of exchanges must be promoted. Anytime we can get an American to visit the USSR or a Russian to visit the United States, particularly for longer visits, we must seize the opportunity. What if thirty years ago Ronald Reagan had had the opportunity to spend one semester studying in the Soviet Union and Leonid Brezhnev had had the chance to spend one semester studying in the United States — what a totally different climate we might have today. That small effort might spell the difference between conflagration and civilization. Bad or good relations between countries rarely result from one large dramatic gesture.

How can we avoid continuation of the arms race between the United States and the USSR?

Moving toward understanding is part of it. But there is more.

In the military a series of options confronts decision makers, just as you face a series of options when you shop at a grocery store. Some options are nutritious and some loaded with calories. Some military options threaten the Soviets and increase their fears, causing them to spend more on armaments, which in turn causes us to spend more on armaments, a spiral that continues upward. Other options improve our military capability but are not viewed by the Soviets as threatening. For example, faced with a choice of an air base in Iran (using a most unlikely scenario), which is on the Soviet border, or using the same money to buy more training time for U.S. pilots on existing bases, training pilots would not be viewed with alarm by the Soviets while building an air base in Iran would, thus escalating the arms race.

Faced with a choice of an MX missile system or a draft, either of which would theoretically strengthen U.S. defenses, the draft would not be viewed as a threat to their homeland; the MX system would.

If our choice is more ammunition for existing weaponry or sending two more divisions to Germany, the former they can understand, the latter they cannot.

The announcement that the neutron bomb will be produced is one of those choices. According to news accounts, Defense Secretary Caspar Weinberger won out in this decision in an intra-administration struggle with Secretary of State Alexander Haig. (It is one of those ironies in government that civilians often seem to feel the necessity to sound tougher than the generals.) Its production and possible use lowers the threshold of nuclear war; the Germans are badly divided on whether they want it in their country, and since it is an antitank weapon that could only conceivably be used against the Soviets, without German cooperation the weapon is completely meaningless;

and we already have extremely effective antitank weapons. The decision to proceed appears to be more politically than militarily motivated. And not surprisingly, a few days after the announcement the Soviets announced they were moving ahead to develop a neutron weapon. The end result of our announcement will only be a world less safe.

We should constantly be aware that, if our choices frighten the Soviets into greater arms expenditures, then those expenditures are at least in part counterproductive.

What are our military-manpower problems?

We have a quality problem, a quantity problem, and a utilization problem.

"There is a substantial problem in slippage in the caliber of our officers," a top military leader who had just retired told me at a small dinner party. The next day I read that our tank gunners, in target competition with other NATO countries, scored at the bottom. In 1964, 13.9 percent of those in the army had some college; now it is 3.2 percent and declining. Over and over and over I hear tales about incompetence, about sophisticated weaponry operated by personnel not equipped to handle it. Training manuals for the armed forces have had to be rewritten to what some call "the comic-book level" in order to reach the new recruits, and even then many cannot comprehend them.

There is a quantity problem now in getting recruits and in holding middle-level personnel. The air force is short thirteen hundred pilots. The army is now short forty-seven thousand noncommissioned officers, the navy twenty-two thousand. Those who are in the service, as a result, are often overworked. The failure to meet recruitment quotas is going to become a much greater problem — if and when the economy improves — aggravated by a drop of approximately one-fourth in the number of people in the prime-recruitment age in the next decade. The most casual glance at the numbers problem suggests substantial changes in policy must be made. By the end of the decade, the services will have to recruit one out of three noncollege males in order to meet the present anticipated goals, a most unlikely scenario.

Utilization of personnel already in the service is also a problem. Pilots are receiving fewer hours in the air than all experts agree is desirable to achieve combat effectiveness. Because of shortages of ammunition, few personnel have sufficient opportunity to practice with live ammunition, particularly with the highly sophisticated weaponry. Our attention to the exotic weapons system is cutting back on the nuts and bolts of basic military-personnel readiness.

How do we solve the military-manpower problems?

The problem of recruitment must be solved by some form of the draft. The draft will not be a reality for perhaps another four years, but it is coming, regardless of who promises what, because of the statistical realities. I favor a draft that offers all Americans at the age of eighteen, or following high-school graduation, the choice of a year in the military with special educational benefits for those who follow that path, or a year in the Peace Corps or VISTA or on the staff of a mental hospital, a park district, a school, or any one of perhaps one hundred choices. Every American would understand that at that age he or she would owe the country one year. I favor this because:

• A draft would help solve our military-personnel problems.

• A draft would make service in the armed forces more equitable. Now, primarily the poor are entering, and if blood is to be shed, it will be the poor who will bear that burden. That kind of economic sanction fundamentally violates what we as a nation ought to stand for.

• A draft would be a restraint on the use of force. If only those in the lower-income brackets suffer — those who tend to be less articulate politically — and if the sons and daughters of members of Congress and the members of the Cabinet are not involved, it becomes easier to use force. I want great care taken before force is used. If we had not had the student deferment during the Vietnam conflict, we would have been out of there sooner. By providing substantial educational benefits to those who go into the military, there is reason to believe that significant numbers of those of middle- and upper-income families would choose the one year of military service. Representative Paul McCloskey, a Republican from California, has reported polling results among young people supporting that contention.

• A draft would speak to another national need: far too many young people who are functionally illiterate could be helped during this one-year period. Illiteracy is at an intolerably high level. Other industrial nations do not experience this phenomenon and it is hurting the United States as well as these people.

• A draft is a safeguard to freedom. One of the lessons of history is that a professional army is too easily talked into "safeguarding" a country by moving in and taking over. We have a marvelous tradition of civilian control of the military. We should keep it that way. An infusion of nonprofessionals into the armed services is a safeguard.

• A year of service to the country would strengthen the nation in many ways. Those who go on to college would be more mature. Those who have minimal proficiencies but are not high-school graduates could be encouraged to use that year to improve their skills along with their service. And those who serve, in whatever capacity, would find their year working in a mental hospital or a park personally rewarding.

Should we proceed with the second phase of the Strategic Arms Limitations Talks (SALT II)?

The only alternative to arms agreements is endless escalation of the arms conflict, and that clearly imperils our security. There are two points which should be kept in mind:

1. Most forms of arms development are verifiable today. Not only do the United States and the Soviet Union have the usual intelligence sources, which are getting better on both sides, but satellites give us unbelievable details about each other. For example, we can tell when missiles are deployed and the nature of those missiles. Camera and other forms of surveillance from the air cannot tell us about stockpiles of chemical weapons, but many forms of military strength are observable, including troop movements. To fail to achieve an arms agreement would be particularly shortsighted in a world in which each side has an amazing ability to know what the other side is doing.

2. The need for arms control can hardly be exaggerated. In the fall of 1980 a Titan II missile exploded and the warhead fell into a wooded section of Arkansas still intact, unexploded. The newspapers reported that the missile had a nine-megaton warhead. That was meaningless to almost everyone. What is a megaton? When a car or bus blows up in El Salvador or Northern Ireland, ordinarily one to five pounds of TNT causes the damage. A megaton is the equivalent of a freight train three hundred miles long loaded with TNT; a

nine-megaton warhead is the equivalent of a freight train twenty-seven hundred miles long (almost the width of the country) loaded with TNT. It is power of such dimensions that we cannot adequately comprehend it. That nine-megaton warhead is smaller than some and one of only thousands that we and the Soviets (and, in smaller quantities, a few other nations) have. All of the bombs of World War II, including those at Hiroshima and Nagasaki, totaled approximately two megatons in power. The explosion of only one of the larger nuclear weapons over a major city would cause more deaths than the United States has experienced in any war, including the Civil War. Talk about surviving a nuclear war is talk that ignores reality. Agreement with the Soviets is not a luxury; it is a necessity.

Let me return to an earlier point. Security must be viewed from a much broader perspective. President Eisenhower recognized this when, during his presidency, he stated: "Every gun that is made, every warship launched, every rocket fired signifies, in the final sense, a theft from those who hunger and are not fed, those who are cold and not clothed."[5] The Vatican said much the same in a message to the United Nations: "The waste involved in the overproduction of military devices . . . is an act of aggression which amounts to a crime, for even when they are not used, by their cost alone armaments kill the poor by causing them to starve."[6]

One of the keen budget watchers until his retirement, Henry Bellmon, then a Republican senator from Oklahoma, commented: "We no longer possess the economic resources to fund national security in an undirected fashion, and still adequately meet domestic spending priorities and keep inflation under control. We cannot afford unlimited guns and plentiful butter. . . . We need to know what defense does responsibly require."[7]

In his memoirs — which are still not available to the Soviet public — Nikita Khrushchev relates a conversation he had with President Eisenhower:

> "Tell me, Mr. Khrushchev, how do you decide on funds for military expenditures? . . . Perhaps first I should tell you how it is with us. . . . It's like this. My military leaders come to me and say, 'Mr. President, we need such and such a sum for such and such a program. If we don't get the funds we need, we'll fall behind the Soviet Union.' So invariably I

give in. That's how they wring money out of me. They keep grabbing for more, and I keep giving it to them. Now tell me, how is it with you?"

"It's just the same. Some people from our military department come and say, 'Comrade Khrushchev, look at this! The Americans are developing such and such a system. We could develop the same system but it would cost such and such.' I tell them there's no money; it's been allotted already. So they say, 'If we don't get the money we need and there's a war, then the enemy will have superiority over us.' So we talk about it some more; I mull over their request and finally come to the conclusion that the military should be supported with whatever funds they say they need. Then I put the matter to the government and we take the steps which our military people have recommended."

"Yes," he said, "that's what I thought. You know we really should come to some sort of an agreement in order to stop this fruitless, really wasteful rivalry."[8]

CHAPTER FOURTEEN

Foreign Policy

President William McKinley wrote in 1898: "The mission of the United States is one of benevolent assimilation."[1] Eighteen months later the Democratic platform of 1900 said: "We assert that no nation can long endure half republic and half empire, and we warn the American people that imperialism abroad will lead quickly and inevitably to despotism at home."

There have been times in our history when foreign policy has been a matter of sharp dispute and other times when the nation effectively pulled together. Our present status is somewhere in between. But there is no area where a political party should be more careful in defining its role, for what is at stake can literally be civilization itself. Where President Reagan is right, we should support him; where he is wrong — though popular in that wrong position — we should responsibly oppose him.

Several broad principles should guide our foreign policy, none of them startlingly new in the history of nations, but they are not always easily adhered to.

We should be firm but not bellicose, strong but sensitive. The countries of Western Europe, Japan, and other nations should look to the United States as a solid upholder of peace, a strong bulwark against Soviet or any other type of aggression. It is particularly important that the NATO countries feel they have a strong shield in the United States, a nation that can use its power if necessary to protect the Western Alliance.

But equally important, they should know that we will not flex our muscles unnecessarily. The United States has generally been looked to as a source of stability and security by Western Europe. That is still the case, although increasing numbers there question our stability and view us as almost as great a threat to their security as the Soviets. It is not that they think we would ever invade, but they read about statements the president makes that they recognize as great for U.S. domestic politics but not for the cause of peace. They view us as diplomatically immature; they believe we view the world as one great western movie where we are the good guys and the Soviets are the villains. This is not to suggest that the Western European nations do not appreciate freedom, nor that they are about to embrace the Soviet system with its denials of basic human rights. But they also recognize that nations operate from a perspective of self-interest regardless of their political system and that national leaders in any system say things that please "the home folks" and sometimes jeopardize international relations in the process. Various Western leaders have said that, although they do not approve of the Soviet system, the West and East are "doomed to coexist with one another." President Reagan says the Soviets reserve to themselves "the right to commit any crime, to lie, to cheat" in order to reach their goals. He won't lose any votes at home saying that, but does that make the Soviets more open to serious negotiation?

I happened to be in the Soviet Union shortly after the president, in response to a press-conference question, said that not only the news from Poland, but "the reports that are beginning to come out of Russia itself . . . [are] an indication that communism is an aberration. . . . [This is] the beginning of the end."[2] And then Secretary of State Alexander Haig reinforced that: "I think we are witnessing a historic unraveling of Marxism-Leninism on the Soviet model."[3] If they are both right, then why spend all that money on defense? And if they are right, why say it and needlessly offend a major military power? And if they are wrong, why say it? The Soviet leaders inherit not only the Communist ideology, but also the leadership mantle of a nation that, historically, Western European nations viewed as culturally deprived and second-rate. Because of that the Soviets have great sensitivity to perceived insults. They are proud of their country. You can imagine how we might react if President Brezhnev had said that the United States is falling apart at the seams, that we are coming to our finale. Should we expect the Soviets to react any differently? Leaders of nations should not express every thought they have, particularly if it makes the pursuit of peace more difficult. The Soviets want to be respected. We should give them that respect. Doing so is not a sign of weakness.

We should be tactful but firm in standing for freedom and human rights. One of the genuinely fine foreign-affairs thrusts made by President Carter — and there were many — was his stand for human rights. Sometimes we were a little too sanctimonious about it, sometimes a little inept, but the message went out to small villages in remote countries that the president of the United States believed in certain principles that had meaning in their lives. It kindled a spark of hope, and even the most obdurate dictator found himself slightly on the defensive, making at least a few gestures in the right direction. It is fine to say that we will pursue these goals through diplomatic channels, as President Reagan has said, but the clear image abroad is that human rights are less important to this administration, that we are concerned about our freedom but less concerned about the freedom of others. The worst possible example has been provided by Chester Crocker, Reagan's assistant secretary of state for Africa. In South Africa, where the white minority is abusing the black majority, Crocker said that we should not "be forced to align ourselves with one side or another."[4] It is like having said in Hitler's early years that we should not have to choose between the Nazis and the Jews. Columnist Carl Rowan described the statement as "so lacking in morality as to make a jackal puke."[5] The United States should not choose between blacks and whites in South Africa or anywhere else, but we should choose between justice and injustice, and in South Africa that means a strong stand against racial oppression.

Soviet leaders should also understand that those who struggle for freedom of expression and freedom to emigrate have our support and strong sympathy. One of the most memorable evenings I have ever spent was when I visited with the wife of exiled Soviet scientist Andrei Sakharov and the mother of the imprisoned Anatoly Shcharansky, as well as some others in that small band of brave people in Moscow who courageously, and at substantial peril, stand for things we take for granted in the United States. The Soviet leadership does not like to deal with uncertainties. On the human-rights issue any U.S. administration should make clear that the strong sympathies of the people of the United States are with people who strive for freedom in the Soviet Union as elsewhere.

It is true that the human-rights issue sometimes gets sticky. It cannot be pushed with uniform vigor. We are not pleased with what South Korea is doing to the political opposition, for example, but to pull out troops suddenly would destabilize that part of the world. However, we should be nudging nations in the right direction, not with a pious "we are better than you are" attitude, and not with the goal that other nations become carbon copies of the United States — one of our persistent failings. The late shah of Iran wrote with bitterness, but with some truth: "America's postwar history is an uninterrupted demand that the rest of the world resemble America, no matter what the history — political, economic and social — of other nations might have been. The example of Vietnam haunts me still. Unlike the French, who had a sense of what could and could not be done, the U.S. set out to build a new nation in Vietnam modeled on itself."[6] Our goals should be limited, but we should speak as friend to friend, letting others know honestly what we believe, and why, on the matter of human rights.

We should not fool ourselves into equating military power with diplomatic power. There is a line running through much of the Reagan-Haig-Weinberger dialogue that suggests that if we could once again achieve military "superiority" we could expect more diplomatic victories. It is a misreading of history. We should maintain an adequate military, recognize that it will provide a shield for which many nations will be grateful, but that will rarely translate into diplomatic victories. In fact, the Soviet arms buildup teaches the opposite lesson. When we were, by any gauge, vastly superior to the Soviets militarily, they moved in to dominate policy making in Egypt, Sudan, Indonesia, Cuba, Somalia, and several smaller countries; in all of those except Cuba they have lost their influence since they have become much more powerful militarily. At one time China was considered as much a Soviet satellite as Bulgaria; but growing Soviet might did not help maintain that situation. Poland is the most dramatic recent example of partial drift; Hungary is in a quiet way showing considerable independence; and Rumania does not permit Soviet troops within her borders and even voted against the Soviet Union in the United Nations on the

Afghanistan question. The Soviets have illustrated that military might cannot be equated with diplomatic success. Military strength may bolster the resolve of friendly nations, but it is no substitute for effective, personal diplomacy.

Both the United States and the Soviet Union must adjust to a world where our voices are less dominant. The two nations dominate the world militarily, but economically we are today much more in a world of equals. For example, Japan's gross national product now probably exceeds the Soviet Union's. This economic slippage means that other nations, including Third World countries, feel no necessity to fall into either camp and may resent our pushing them. Public-opinion polls show that Americans do not recognize this new economic reality; business inattention to export possibilities suggests that far too many American businesses do not understand the world of 1982; and too often a phrase dropped here and there by U.S. officials (including people in Congress) suggests that they do not understand that the world of 1982 is vastly different from the world of 1952. It may hurt our pride to acknowledge a decline in economic dominance, but this reality may reduce the likelihood of armed confrontation between the two military superpowers. President Reagan made the right decision in attending the "meeting with the Third World," a gathering of twenty-three heads of state that took place late in 1981 in Cancun, Mexico. The meeting had to be helpful to all of the chief executives. Increasingly, when there is a "power" meeting at an international level, it will involve more than the traditional major powers. That, on balance, will be good.

We should remember our friends. I have always felt less than happy about the way the United States handled the shah of Iran after his removal from power. I'm not sure what should have been done, and I was no great fan of the shah, but I admired the way President Sadat stood up and I felt uneasy that we had not. I fear that we conveyed a willingness to use people but not befriend them. The Taiwan-China switch was handled less than graciously, perhaps in the long run even dangerously. I have long felt we should recognize China; to fail to do so was totally unrealistic. But probably we could have done it on our terms if we had had patience, as we did with the two Germanys. Taiwan has performed some economic miracles. It is not a bastion of freedom, but it has substantially more freedom than the mainland does; it did not deserve to be pushed into a diplomatic ashcan. On top of that, we indicated that the Taiwan-China issue is an internal matter trust this new friend understands that any attempt to take over Taiwan by military means will cause a severe strain on United States-China relations.

The cold shoulder we have given Algeria is something that defies belief. Algeria played *the* decisive role in securing the release of our hostages from Iran. Having played a small part in convincing Algeria to get involved, I was pleased to see that government greatly extend itself, with Foreign Minister Mohamed Seddick Benyahia and others devoting long hours and a huge amount of time to working out the hostage release. Algeria's ambassador to the United States, Redha Malek, also played an important role in all of this. They were thanked profusely by Under Secretary of State Warren Christopher and by U.S. officials of every stripe from the president on down. They were told we would be "forever grateful" to them. A few months later their neighbor and our friend, Morocco, requested arms. Morocco and Algeria have a dispute in the western Sahara over the independence of that territory, but the United States provided the weapons to Morocco without so much as consulting Algeria. Supplying weapons in itself was a mistake and also not a favor for Morocco, in my opinion, but if policy makers felt it essential, then Algeria should have been consulted. Our memory is short. It was an opportune time to improve relations with a country where there has been a strain. Algeria obviously felt good about what it had done to help us with the hostages. We have mishandled a magnificent opportunity. And what message do we convey to other countries? It is still not too late to have a White House dinner expressing appreciation to Algeria. These gestures are important.

Old allies should not be neglected either. Israel, because of that beleaguered nation's position, must be reassured regularly of our friendship, both for her sake and so that no neighbor miscalculates. We too easily take for granted Canada and Mexico, both of which are sensitive, major powers.

We should understand that no nation has too many friends. I hesitate to belabor the obvious, but the obvious is not apparent to those who call the shots at the Office of Management and Budget (OMB). They issue papers about "nations of lesser importance" in Asia and Africa, and the budget reflects that same insensitivity. As dollars become tight, OMB suggests that international-exchange programs, such as the for China. Does that mean that China can invade Taiwan without our protest? I am pleased with our new relationship with China, but I Fulbright fellowships, should be cut back more than 50 percent — an incredibly shortsighted policy engineered by people who do not understand the world today. When William McKinley was president that might have been a barely tolerable policy, but to fail to take steps to create understanding in the world eight decades later is incomprehensible.

The problem does not rest solely at the feet of the executive branch. Congress must take its share of the blame, along with the media and the public. Congress must assume blame because we have not devised a system to ensure that within a period of a few years all nations are visited by at least one member of the House or Senate. An ambassador from a small nation in Africa told me that no one from the Congress has visited his country in sixteen years. A South American ambassador told me the only member to visit his country has been one of Congress's highly publicized right-wing members. Major nations, who understand the importance of Congress in our decision-making process, do not have a congressional visitor for several years. Members of Congress ought to be traveling more, not less, but we should be planning our trips with more care. The Paris Air Show, France's annual international display of the latest in aviation, is probably important, but a few less members there and more to Bangladesh and Guatemala and Uruguay and Surinam and a host of other seldom-visited countries would do the nation more good.

The media must also be faulted, first for declining coverage of foreign affairs at a point in history when what happens elsewhere affects us more and more. And almost equally important, the media must be faulted for failure to create a climate in which travel abroad is a political necessity for a member of Congress. A lawmaker who does not travel overseas at least once a year is simply not doing his or her job. Yet anyone in the House or Senate knows that there almost always will be some unfavorable response to overseas travel, but rarely an editorial expressing approval. I have yet to read an editorial in any newspaper anywhere criticizing a member for not traveling. They should be written. For a member of the House or Senate to vote regularly on the problems of Korea, or the Middle East, or on our relations with the Warsaw Pact nations without ever having visited, without ever having gotten a feel of the situation, without ever having noticed the minutiae you can only get from a visit — this is stupid and irresponsible. But, politically, it is an asset. I have seen political literature saying that "X has been in Congress twelve years and has never taken a trip abroad." That member ought to receive an editorial blistering, but he or she never does. And so Congress sometimes makes myopic decisions, often on the basis of an amendment introduced by someone who knows almost nothing about the situation to which the amendment applies, but with the full knowledge that the amendment will play well in the media back home. And uninformed members, afraid of the media back home, too often accept the amendment.

Yes, there are trips where there is abuse of the travel privilege, and that should be stopped. But the great abuse is *not* traveling; the great abuse is making decisions that have tremendous impact on the economic health and security of this nation and other nations without the knowledge on which to base these decisions.

One of the areas where significant strides were made under the Carter administration was Africa. We are going back to our old ways under the Reagan administration. What could save us in Africa are a few members of Congress such as Representatives Stephen Solarz of New York and Howard Wolpe of Michigan who have visited extensively, understand the situation, and may prevent the nation from stumbling too much.

Where we cannot take large steps toward mutual accommodation, we should take small ones. Large, dramatic breakthroughs in relations with the Soviets and others are welcome, but often the small unheralded gestures on both sides are much more important. No significant change in our relationship with Albania, to use an extreme example, is likely to occur, but we should be asking ourselves: Are there small steps that can be taken quietly to improve relationships between our two countries, or at least between individuals of our two countries? Perhaps a member of Congress should visit Albania, as soon as that is possible. If no U.S. official is welcomed there, at least the U.S. ambassador in some other country where Albania maintains an embassy could invite the Albanian ambassador and his wife to dinner. The State Department should, on a country-by-country basis, be asking itself what steps can be taken to improve relations. There is no country where improved relations are not possible. There is no country where at least small steps toward friendship cannot be taken.

Our decisions in foreign affairs should reflect the national interest, not the national passion. It is easy to serve the national passion; it is much more difficult to serve the national interest. Cuba and Vietnam are illustrations of the problem.

If you count Lithuania, Estonia, Latvia, and Mongolia as, tragically, almost incorporated into the Soviet Union, then among the other Communist nations there are only two that, no matter how tortuous the path or what the situation, virtually always will be with the Soviets: Bulgaria and Cuba, with East Germany and Czechoslovakia in a tie for third. If you were to sit down in Moscow and decide how you could design U.S. foreign policy so that Cuba would remain close to the bosom of the Soviet Union, you could not have devised a better policy than the one that has emerged — nor worse from the U.S. position. United States politicians can make anti-Castro speeches and stay in office, and that permits Castro to make anti–United States speeches and stay in office. We should be trying to woo Cuba away from the Soviet orbit. Castro himself is sensitive to the charge that Cuba has become a Soviet satellite; he has pointed out that Cuba disagreed with the Soviets on the Law of the Sea treaty — an illustration of Cuba's potential for independence, rather than proof of its independence. Would any great harm be done to the United States, for example, if we decided to sell medicine and food to Cuba? Isn't it better from the viewpoint of U.S. policy that these things come from us rather than the Soviet Union? There is no guarantee that gestures of friendship will modify Cuban policy, but there is a guarantee that the present policy can only result in Cuba's continued close and reverential attachment to the USSR.

Senator Paul Tsongas of Massachusetts has correctly noted: "The brilliant strategists who called for the end of Castro through isolation are immune from criticism. The policy has been a blunder of monumental proportions, serving only the interests of the Soviets, and yet the architects of that policy and its present-day adherents are never questioned. It is one of the few instances in American foreign policy-making where nothing succeeds quite like failure."[7]

After World War II the United States had the good fortune to have as our president Harry Truman. Despite considerable criticism, he extended the hand of friendship to Japan and Germany. They are now among our strongest allies. After the Vietnam War, the government of Hanoi initially did not want to enter into diplomatic relations with the United States until we worked out what they felt was a commitment from President Nixon for $3 billion to rebuild that war-ravaged nation. The United States was in no mood for such a settlement. In 1978 the door opened again, and this time the Vietnamese government indicated in an informal meeting with some members of the House, Senate, and State Department that Vietnam would like to enter into diplomatic relations and trade with the United States. They made clear that they wanted to chart a course independent of both China and the Soviet Union, but that was becoming increasingly difficult. The Soviets wanted to use the great naval facility at Cam Ranh Bay that the United States had built, but up to that point Vietnam had not approved the Soviet move. That evening-long bipartisan meeting broke up with the feeling that we would move ahead. We felt we were at the beginning of a new era in our relationship with Vietnam, the world's third most populous Communist nation. But someone at the White House vetoed the idea, perhaps out of fear of China's reaction, perhaps out of fear of the domestic political reaction. Our ambassador to the United Nations, Andrew Young, later told me that he did not think Vietnam would have invaded Cambodia (Kampuchea) had the United States recognized Vietnam. Under pressure from the Soviets, the Vietnamese apparently felt they had lost their chance to establish a more independent base through ties with the United States. We cannot rerun history, but if it is in our national interest to have Vietnam as independent as possible from the two major Communist powers — and it clearly is — then our policy should reflect that reality; it does not. Now the invasion of Cambodia has complicated matters, but some type of quid pro quo in which the United States would recognize Vietnam and Vietnam would agree to gradually withdraw troops from Cambodia would appear to be in the interests of all parties.

As of the time of this writing, the dust has not settled from the exchange of fire between Libyan and American planes in which two

Libyan fighters were shot down. But columnist Carl Rowan has addressed the thoughtful national-interest questions that I hope someone within the administration considered before we put "the chip on our shoulder." No nation recognizes Libya's unilateral claim to sovereignty over the Gulf of Sidra. Rowan knows that Libyan strongman Colonel Qaddafi is supplied weapons by the Soviets and is not a pillar of stability, but adds: "We must note that Moscow does not yet have military bases in Libya, and it does not control Libya's important petroleum reserves. Qaddafi did, while in Russia, say that the Soviets should get out of Afghanistan and that Poland must remain free. Wouldn't it be an outrage if the Soviets wound up with Libyan bases and Libya's oil simply because the United States decided to demonstrate its 'muscle' in the Gulf of Sidra? What kind of foreign policy is this where we vow we'll go to war, spilling the blood of thousands of Americans, to insure that the Soviets do not grasp control of the oil fields of the Persian Gulf area when at the same time we try to 'give' Russia the oil fields of Libya, forty percent of whose production comes to this country? A wise foreign policy does not permit today's emotions, or political needs, to obscure America's imperatives of tomorrow."[8]

We should learn the lessons of recent history, particularly in Vietnam. There are many things to be learned from the Vietnam tragedy, but these three are important:

1. We should know more about the rest of the world. When we got involved in Vietnam there were fewer than five American-born specialists in our entire country who understood any of the languages or the culture of that area. The United States made earth-shaking decisions on the basis of paper-thin knowledge. We don't know where difficulties may arise tomorrow, so "saving money" by not educating ourselves on the languages and background of a country or an area can be extremely costly.

2. In a democracy it is difficult to sustain long-term troop involvement in an area far from our borders. The temporary spirit of patriotism and wave of euphoria give way as casualty figures mount.

3. Military commitments should be prudently made, for neither our resources nor our spirit are unlimited. "The United States cannot be the policeman for the world" was a sentence we often heard after Vietnam, but hear much less today. There is a sensible middle ground

between that position and one of isolationism in military commitments. I fear we are now tilted toward excessive military
commitments.

We should be willing to talk to anyone. Prior to the shah's fall, at his
request the American embassy had no contact with the National Front
and other opposition forces. Our failure to talk with them was no
favor to the shah, and it hurt us also. For several years U.S. embassies
in North Africa had orders not to talk to anyone from the Polisario,
the group that is involved in a struggle for independence in the
western Sahara. We took this stand at the request of the king of
Morocco, an old friend of the United States who runs a remarkably
free nation by African standards. Again, by divorcing our embassies
from reality, we have helped neither the king nor our government.
Fortunately, that policy of noncontact has changed. I was an admirer
of President Sadat of Egypt. History will probably record him as one
of the giants of this century. But our refusal to talk to his opposition in
Egypt, at that government's request, again was — and is — unsound
policy. We should be willing to talk to the Palestine Liberation
Organization (PLO). The United States could continue to honor
Henry Kissinger's pledge not to enter into formal negotiations with
the PLO, but maintain informal contact. There will be no permanent
settlement of the Middle East situation until the Palestinian question is
resolved, and rightly or wrongly, the Palestinians regard the PLO as
their voice. When I was in Damascus, I talked to one of the top PLO
leaders, but the U.S. embassy there is under orders not to engage in
such conversation. We do neither Israel nor ourselves a favor by
refusing to talk. I would not recognize them; I would not invite them
to dinners at the embassy; but talk and listen, yes! Talking and
listening rarely do any harm if engaged in judiciously, and sometimes
talking and listening can prevent shooting.

As much as possible, we should talk to others in their language. Our
foreign service and overseas military both need substantial
strengthening. Of our 52 hostages in Iran, 6 spoke Farsi, 2 of the 6
fluently. Of 488,000 armed-service personnel stationed overseas, 412
are recognized by the service as linguistically competent. An
interesting experiment is about to take place. We have demonstration
projects for everything imaginable, so with the help of my colleagues
in the House and Senate I placed an amendment on the Foreign

Service Act that requires the Secretary of State to make a demonstration project of "at least two" non-English-speaking countries where everyone on the embassy staff, including the secretaries and the marine guards, are required to speak the language of the country in which they are stationed. The nations selected are Uruguay and Senegal. We may be surprised at the result. The day must soon pass when U.S. embassy personnel live in comfortable isolation from the people of the country in which they are stationed, all, that is, except the well educated who speak English. Aloofness and arrogance are not the qualities we want to convey, but too often that is exactly what we do. An article on the energy problem noted: "Americans find themselves depending on peoples — Saudis, Mexicans, Nigerians — to whom they have always felt superior and, therefore, do not understand very well."[9] That must change. All of this is related to the quality question. Can the United States have the quality of Foreign Service it wants if it is almost the only diplomatic service in the world that does not require some type of foreign-language competence before entry? The status of our diplomatic corps in this regard reflects the status of our culture. The American people do not speak other languages and so we have dropped this requirement for diplomats. An improvement in language skills is needed by both the public and the diplomatic corps.

We should not read an East-West struggle into every incident in every country. Our blunders in this area are legion and go back through many administrations. When you face an ideological foe, as we do in the Soviets, it is risky not to assume Soviet involvement; but sometimes paranoia takes over and warps our view of a situation. That can cause policy blunders. What the newly independent nations want is what they have achieved: independence. They worship neither at Moscow's shrine nor at Washington's. If we are rebuffed from time to time, it does not mean the Soviets have another conquest. Because we overdo the East-West confrontation, too often we are perceived as being against social justice. Those who want social justice are not necessarily Communists. Sometimes they are, and sometimes those who make the loudest speeches about social justice have little interest in it and are only lackeys of the Soviets. Each situation should be analyzed carefully. We should not be unmindful of the Soviet threat, but an overly simplistic approach to these situations does us harm.

Our overreaction causes embarrassment to our friends. When the French sent officials to Central America, one French diplomat commented about the delegation: "They have got to walk a thin line between their commitment to social justice and their desire for a working relationship with the United States."[10] That does sound strange. Our aim should continually be to permit nations to choose their own course. When they do that, their concerns quickly become practical and economic, rather than ideological, and the West has more to offer by way of example of economic progress than do our Soviet competitors. If we offer steady, solid cooperation — and tolerate some different approaches — we will not see many Soviet-dominated nations emerging. United Nations Ambassador Andrew Young, at the close of his term, commented: "To keep what we have gained [in Africa] we must avoid a return to East-West analysis of events in Africa; that would return us to the days — only four short years ago — when American influence on the continent was at its lowest. Instead, a wise policy will continue to emphasize aggressive diplomacy, based on a clear perception of African political sensibilities."[11] That's good advice for any area of the world.

Finally, and by no means least important, the spark of compassion for the world's desperate must return to a much more dominant role in U.S. foreign policy. One of our distinguished senior statesmen, Clark Clifford, former secretary of defense and confidant of several presidents, said recently: "If there is any one statement I have read that has given me a deep sense of gratification, it was a statement by one of the leading historians . . . of the twentieth century, Arnold Toynbee. . . . Toynbee said when history looks back on the twentieth century, the greatest development of the century will not be the discovery of nuclear or atomic energy. It will be the act of one of the great powers in the world, with no expectation of recompense, to lean down and help other nations of the world rebuild so that they might maintain their own freedom."[12]

When the Marshall Plan was in full effect we spent 2.9 percent of our gross national product to help the poor beyond our borders. Now we are spending less than one-fifth of 1 percent, less than Japan or any Western European nation except for Spain and Italy. Why the change? Under the Marshall Plan, your House and Senate members could go home and tell the Schmidts, "I'm helping your relatives in

Germany." They could tell the Scarianos, "I'm helping your relatives in Italy." They could tell the Thompsons, "I'm helping your relatives in Great Britain." And so on. There was political mileage in providing help. But now the people who need help live in places like Bangladesh and Chad. People do not come up to me in my southern Illinois district and ask if I'm helping their relatives in Chad. The political mileage is gone. And any Republican or Democrat can stand before an audience anywhere and bluster loudly: "Let's stop sending money down the drain overseas. Let's keep it at home." There will be cheers from the less thoughtful in that audience.

That is the political reality today. But it can be turned around. Economically, my district is the poorest congressional district in the state of Illinois; yet when I ask people if they want to help hungry people in other countries, the answer is inevitably yes. The American people want to do the right thing, but they have heard so many people talk about the abuses of aid — and there have been some — that they have a totally distorted picture of what has happened; they are largely unaware of the tremendous amount of good our foreign economic assistance has done. They are also unaware that most economic assistance actually is spent in the United States on food and fertilizers, tractors and plows, the items Third World countries need to increase their ability to help themselves. And there is a grossly exaggerated picture of how much is spent.

There are practical economic reasons for assisting those beyond our borders: as their standard of living improves they become customers for our products. Our most rapidly growing markets are in the developing, not the developed, nations. Approximately 40 percent of U.S. overseas sales are now with the developing nations — more than with Western Europe, Japan, Australia, New Zealand, and South Africa combined. There is also a practical political reason for assistance. Although there are a number of exceptions, it is generally true that the United States is interested in stability, and the Soviets welcome instability as an opportunity to achieve their ends. If we can improve the lives of the impoverished in the developing nations so that they do not feel a revolution of some kind is necessary, that generally serves our political ends. That reality is fairly obvious, yet most of our Republican colleagues in Congress, and some of our Democrats, have not understood this. They believe a submarine fights Soviet aims; they do not understand that if you give people hope and opportunity, that also does. If we take the humanitarian action, we can avoid what Sir Francis Bacon called "the rebellions of the belly."[13]

In 1974 the World Food Conference called upon all governments to accept as a goal that in ten years' time no child would go to bed hungry and no family would fear for its food for the next day. That goal is more distant now than it was in 1974. John Gilligan, the former director of the Agency for International Development (AID), has pointed out that more than 15 million children under the age of five die each year because of malnutrition or diseases brought on by malnutrition. That, he noted, is the equivalent of a Hiroshima-type bomb dropping every third day for one year — only the victims are all under five and all these deaths could be prevented.[14] The 1981 report of the World Bank predicts bleakly: "The income gap between the richest and poorest countries will continue to increase." A few months after he became president, Jimmy Carter spoke at Notre Dame: "Abraham Lincoln said that our nation could not exist half-slave and half-free. We know that a peaceful world cannot long exist one-third rich and two-thirds hungry."[15]

If instead of some of the military assistance we send abroad we could provide more economic assistance, if the spark of warmth and enthusiasm could be returned to what we do beyond our borders, it would not only be of great help to much of humanity that cannot even dream of things we take for granted, but it would renew the symbol of the United States as a nation that cares. We have lost much of that. If the American flag stood for that to people in other nations, there might not have been hostages taken in Iran. Too often we now convey an image of being big, rich, powerful, and unconcerned. President Carter had the right instincts in this area, and I once talked to him about having a "fireside chat" with the nation on this subject. He expressed some interest in the idea, though I don't know whether or not he ever seriously considered it. It is still a good idea. When John F. Kennedy got on television and told the nation why he was using U.S. marshals to insure that James Meredith could go to school in Mississippi, he moved us. A president who would lead the nation in helping the world's poor and tells us why this is in our own long-range interest would be doing this nation and the world a great favor. We like to do good things. We like to be proud of ourselves. And particularly on foreign affairs, the American people are willing to be led. On Vietnam, the public eventually turned against the administration; but ordinarily the public will follow, especially when the leadership appeals to humanitarian instincts.

The reasons for action are growing. There will be another two billion people on the face of the earth in less than twenty years. I once debated former Secretary of Agriculture Earl Butz (an interesting experience in itself), and in response to a question from the audience, Butz said that if you counted all the people who have lived on the face of the earth since the beginning of time, the majority are alive today. That is an astounding statistic. Whether it is accurate is difficult to prove or disprove, but we know that, although progress has been made, serious malnutrition is still the lot of at least 500 million people; the majority of people alive today will die before their natural time from some cause related either to lack of food or to lack of protein in their food; most people on the face of the earth today never in their lives will have a meal like your best meal today — and that holds true even if you are a student, complaining about meals in your dormitory. And the United States, with 5 percent of the world's population, produces one-sixth of the world's food and is responsible for more than half of the world grain exports.

The United States should be perceived as more concerned about the misery that is much of humanity's lot. We will be perceived that way when we *are* more concerned. In the last thirty years the United States and the Soviet Union have spent approximately $2 *trillion* on weapons and defense. What kind of a world could we help create if we spent a small percentage of that to bring health and opportunity for self-advancement to the world's miserable!

CHAPTER FIFTEEN

Presidential Selection

T he Democratic party has no shortage of problems. Democrats in Congress take away the muscle from the leadership and then criticize the leadership for not being strong. Republicans, as of 1981, were raising twelve dollars for the 1982 campaign for each dollar the Democrats were raising. Democrats seem to enjoy intraparty fights more than the Republicans do; by nature, Democrats seem to have more passion and exuberance and fun — and chaos. But the process by which the Democratic presidential nominee is selected is so seriously flawed that it needs to be changed.

For a good portion of our history, parties sought the candidate for president rather than the other way around. Even the nation's one pre-political-party president, George Washington, did not seek the presidency. "I most heartily wish the choice to which you allude [election to the presidency] may not fall on me," Washington wrote a friend.[1] Some have refused to run. Sherman's statement to the Republican convention of 1884, "I will not accept if nominated, and will not serve if elected,"[2] is the most famous refusal, though earlier Sherman had put it in even stronger terms: "If forced to choose between the penitentiary and the White House for four years, I would say the penitentiary, thank you."[3]

As you look back upon the stronger presidents each party has produced for the nation prior to 1952, how many would have been willing to go through what we now require of our nominees? The only one I can imagine doing it — and he well might not have — is Theodore Roosevelt. He might have enjoyed it. The list of those eliminated would include George Washington, Thomas Jefferson, Abraham Lincoln, Grover Cleveland, Woodrow Wilson, Franklin D. Roosevelt (who did not do well in the primaries), and Harry Truman.

We are too close to judge the strength of our more recent presidents, but Dwight Eisenhower would not have gone through the process; John Kennedy might have (the primaries were nowhere near as significant in 1960); Lyndon Johnson probably would not have; Richard Nixon might have; Gerald Ford would not have, but for his being named vice president; and Jimmy Carter and Ronald Reagan did go through it.

This really leads to the question of whether we are, through the present process, selecting the wisest and best, those most qualified to lead us. Walter Mondale withdrew as a candidate because after a brief swim in the presidential waters he decided that he did not want to spend a year in Holiday Inns, as he put it. That was to his credit, for the present process virtually requires that the candidate of either party must (1) be unemployed for the two years prior to the election; (2) have a great affinity for endless campaigning in which he learns to evade rather than confront issues; (3) avoid time for thoughtfulness and reflection; and (4) keep his right arm in good shape for handshaking and his smile ready to flash the instant television cameras roll. Perhaps I can be more objective about the Republican party. Had the parliamentary system been in effect in 1980, the Republicans would have chosen Senator Howard Baker or Senator Bob Dole, assuming Senator Lowell Weicker, Representative Phillip Crane, and Representative John Anderson would have been ruled out because of their ideological alignment within the party. The process then — and now — in effect, however, meant that either Baker or Dole would have had to abandon his duties in the Senate to become a viable candidate. My guess is history will judge that either probably would have made a better president than the eventual winner. Of an earlier president an observer commented: "The crowning failure of our system has been made painfully patent in the election of our prime national leader from outside all national and international experience. This is pure, unadulterated folly and we have been witnessing its effects each passing month."[4] That has a timely sound to it.

In 1872 Ulysses S. Grant sought reelection, and unhappy Republicans joined Democrats to nominate Horace Greeley at the Liberal Republican convention. Greeley, who died three weeks after the election, his wife one week before the election, turned out to be a dud of a candidate. But listen to this description of that 1872 convention.

> How then could the convention have nominated the worst possible candidate? Perhaps the answer is that political amateurs assembled to run a national convention of a party without organization represented by delegates without constituencies make political decisions ineffectively. . . . Their collective failure was to hold a convention too open and too fluid to make much sense or serve much purpose. It was spring madness combined with peculiar politics and strange enthusiasm.[5]

That has a disturbingly familiar ring.

In 1976 I served as cochairman of a committee to draft Hubert Humphrey for the Democratic presidential nomination. It started during one night session of the House in 1975. I was sitting around talking with five of my colleagues as we waited for the seemingly endless debate to terminate. Three of them were Democrats, two Republicans. At that point it was not even clear that President Gerald Ford would seek election to the presidency. I asked the five, all of whom are respected members of the House: "Forgetting political party and the whole process of getting elected, if you were able to simply name who the next president should be on the basis that that person would make the best president, whom would you name?" All five named Hubert Humphrey. While I leaned in that direction also, it startled me that there could be this near unanimity among people who really know government, and yet so far as I could see he had no prospect of being the Democratic nominee. A few weeks later I was on a plane with Humphrey and mentioned this conversation. It pleased him, but he said he would do nothing: "They know me. They know what I stand for. If they want me they can get me." Part of this reflected his losing in 1972 when friends urged him to get into the race against a man he greatly respected, George McGovern. Part of it, I believe, was his place in history. "I don't want to be another Harold Stassen," he told me on several occasions. In 1976, through all of those primaries Jimmy Carter was winning, and to his credit worked hard to win, the exit polls conducted consistently showed that had Hubert Humphrey been on the ballot he would have won decisively. But he consistently and stubbornly refused to let his name go on the ballot. The procedure eliminated a man who might have become an outstanding president, though his death in 1978 meant that his term would have been a short one had he been elected.*

In restructuring our nominating process, several changes seem desirable:

The delegates should be free to select the best possible candidate. That is the conclusion of Duke University's president, Terry Sanford, who has studied the process as thoughtfully as anyone and has written a book on it, *A Danger of Democracy: The Presidential Nominating Process.* Sanford comments:

> Eastern Airlines, when looking for a president, could go outside its ranks and pick an astronaut as its chief executive. The Stanford Graduate School of Business could reach into the business world for its dean. Duke University could look at every basketball coach in the country before making an offer to the one it perceived would best serve Duke. The Methodist Church can look at every preacher in the jurisdiction, and at others who are not preachers, when the time comes to elect a bishop. The political party delegates to the national nominating conventions can look at only one or two survivors who have run a crazy obstacle course. I am in favor of delegates who can look at the full field, in order to pick the best possible presidential candidate. Of course that is a radical thought. We need and must have a radical change.[6]

Ordinarily, a delegate will and should vote for the candidate for whom he or she had indicated support prior to being elected or named. But more delegates probably should be elected uncommitted, and those with commitments should be free to change if circumstances change. Polls may show that the original candidate has become a disaster in November; the candidate might be indicted; or someone might emerge who had not been in the primaries, as Adlai Stevenson did in 1952.

---

*It is interesting to speculate what might have happened had Humphrey been the nominee and been elected. On the basis of conversations with him, I believe his choice for vice president, had he emerged early in the process, would have been Representative Morris Udall of Arizona. After Carter had won several primaries, Humphrey indicated that Carter had won the right to that spot, should the delegate vote go to Humphrey. There were several times when he came close to becoming a candidate, the final occasion just before the New Jersey primary filing date. At one point, less than twenty-four hours before the filing deadline, Humphrey told me he would become a candidate, but within hours reversed that decision.

We should have fewer delegates. The convention is in fact more of a rally than a convention. It now simply ratifies what the primaries have already decided. That huge assemblage has little idea what the issues are on which they vote. Those who stay at home and watch the process on television have heard much more of the arguments on both sides than those who will vote at a convention, even though television no longer provides gavel-to-gavel coverage. One House seat in Ohio probably was lost in a special 1981 election because of less than thoughtful platform action by the 1980 Democratic convention.[7] The House of Representatives, with 435 members, is unwieldy and not an ideal body for thoughtful debate; but compared to 3,331 delegates to a political convention, it resembles the Supreme Court.

We should reduce the hoopla and circus atmosphere. I have often heard the following exchange between a returned delegate and a friend: "How was the convention?" "Marvelous! I had a great time." For most delegates, a convention is exactly that: a good time. Milton Eisenhower observed: "A society which insists on running its quadrennial conventions like circuses should not be surprised to get tightrope walkers as presidential candidates."[8] If we want better results at conventions, we would be wise to create an atmosphere that reflects that we are picking a candidate for the most powerful office on earth, someone who literally may hold our fate in his or her hands.

The campaign should be shortened. I am less certain of how it should be done than that it should be done. Regional primaries have been suggested as one alternative, and I am somewhat reluctantly moving toward supporting them as a better alternative than what we have now. The advantage of an Iowa caucus or a New Hampshire primary is that a candidate with limited financial means has a much better chance of emerging than in regional primaries. Perhaps there are ways to overcome that obstacle. We may have to experiment with different alternatives before we find the right one. There is an abundance of studies on possibilities, but few combine the worlds of theory and politics in a realistic way. Some sensible brainstorming should be taking place. If it is not possible to follow a shorter course in 1984 — and I have not given up on that — by all means there should be substantial improvements by 1988. The present lengthy process eliminates thoughtful people who otherwise might become candidates and wearies both the active candidate and the public.

Public officials should have a greater voice in the selection of the nominee and the party platform. Since I am a public official, I speak with some prejudice. In Great Britain and Canada and other parliamentary democracies, almost the total decision is made by the members of Parliament. Until 1824 the "convention" in the United States was a congressional caucus. The change has given the public a much greater voice. But people who are Democratic (or Republican) members of Congress or governors have insights that are important. Of the 3,331 delegates to the Democratic convention of 1980, 45 were members of the House or Senate. Part of that is because our present system discourages members from standing up. Although presidential leadership is the most important decision a party makes every four years, when public officials announce support for a candidate they make a fair number of their constituents unhappy. There is a price to be paid for leadership and most members of Congress and other officials are unwilling to pay it. But their voices should be heard. Stuart Eizenstat, a superb public servant whom Jimmy Carter brought to the White House, has suggested that members of the House and Senate and governors should automatically be delegates. I agree with that suggestion, but under the present procedures, even if they are delegates, the decision has been made on the candidate before the convention, and the platform rarely means anything.

The House and Senate leadership could provide one useful preprimary activity. Let the Democratic (and Republican) members of the House and Senate cast secret ballots prior to the first primary on the person they would like to see as the Democratic nominee. If the American public sees that those involved in government have a clear-cut choice — or do not have one — that might have an impact on the decision by voters in the primary states.

Terry Sanford has said: "The way we pick our presidents should not be fraught with danger and uncertainty. It should be a clear, secure, sensible procedure in which we can have confidence . . ."[9]

And no less an authority than Robert S. Strauss, as insightful a national chairman as the Democratic party probably has ever had, said this during the 1980 campaign: "Perhaps because of my role in the current campaign, this election has taught me more than any other than the methods used to pick a president are flawed, and in need of reform."[10]

CHAPTER SIXTEEN

Becoming a Majority Party Again

My hope is that three needs have become apparent to the readers of this book: for greater compassion, for improved productivity, and for enrichment of the quality of life in every dimension. To the extent the Democratic party is loyal to those goals, it will be a winner whether or not it achieves or maintains majority status, for the party will have served its ultimate purpose — helping the nation.

The postelection Democratic blues of 1980 shifted to a new mood of deep pessimism the first six months of 1981 as the new president seemed to demolish any suggestion of opposition to his programs. But that air of gloom has lifted somewhat and there is a growing awareness that a party, saddled in 1980 with an Iran crisis and inflation, that lost to a man who entered the presidency with less than 51 percent of the vote, should not panic. Elections are won by putting together coalitions, and a winning coalition can emerge in 1982 and in 1984.

Political observer Ben Wattenberg has accurately stated: "Africa is not the only place with tribal politics; we have it in the United States too."[1] He is correct. Labor is one tribe, business is another. Regions are tribes. Religions are tribes. Ethnic groups are tribes. Get enough tribes voting for a party and that party wins.

Wattenberg had another comment of significance: the public image of the Democratic party is that the party is "somewhat unrealistic." What we do in Congress, what we say as a party to those who now are alienated, the platform we adopt in 1984, and how we are perceived on national television long before that platform is adopted — all of these will determine whether we will be viewed as "realistic." Thomas Reed, who served twenty-two years as the Republican Speaker of the House, described the Democratic party in 1892: "A hopeless assortment of discordant differences, as incapable of positive action as it is capable of infinite clamor."[2] There have been times when that has been an accurate description, but far more times when it has not, for our Democratic presidents since that time — Wilson, Roosevelt, Truman, Kennedy, Johnson, and Carter — have generally espoused programs and postures of substance and vision.

But each generation, each decade, each Congress must determine anew whether the Reed description is accurate. "Politics is like roller skating," says political scientist James David Barber. "It takes you in part where you want to go and in part where it takes you."[3] But if you don't know where you want to go or what you are doing, politics, like roller skating, can be dangerous.

If the Democrats move in the direction of a program similar to the one outlined in this book, how would we fare with the various "tribes" that must provide the margin of victory? Here are some comments on a few of these tribes (listed alphabetically):

Blacks: They are strongly Democratic, but often have a low voter turnout. The special election in Mississippi for the seat vacated by Republican U.S. Representative Jon Hinson produced a surprisingly large turnout of black voters, and as a result, an upset Democratic victory for Representative Wayne Dowdy. The Reagan program should give blacks reasons for voting. A good Democratic push toward full employment would help us.

Blue-Collar Workers: Reagan carried a substantial vote here, particularly among nonunion members, but among union members also. Blue-collar workers tend to have conservative social attitudes, but the Reagan tax program helps them little, and the high interest rates hit them hard. A good employment program would increase the Democratic vote. According to the *New York Times*–CBS polls, Carter carried workers concerned about unemployment three to one in 1976 and in 1980 by only 51 to 40 percent.[4]

Business people: Overwhelmingly Republican, they have been barraged with mail from various right-wing groups (often carrying business names), tending to solidify them in the Republican corner. But they are practical people and do not like high interest rates. Increasingly, they sense something is wrong with the

Reagan economic program. They like the Small Business Administration and Farmers Home Administration, both of which Democrats have supported. If business people see Democrats taking action to balance the budget and bring interest rates down, there will be converts. This is particularly true of home builders, automobile dealers, and other businesses highly dependent on interest rates. The jobs program would mean less expenditure by business on unemployment compensation, a matter of no small significance to business people. Democrats need to be reaching them by mailings because they are not hearing the Democratic side now, a sad reality for many other groups also.

Catholics: As prejudice against them has diminished, Roman Catholics increasingly vote as others do. The one issue for some Catholics is abortion, and candidates must try to avoid being inaccurately labeled as proabortion for opposing a constitutional amendment. Catholic bishops do not want to be identified on that issue alone, and have taken strong stands on arms control and other social issues more closely identified with traditional Democratic positions.

Farmers: Generally Republican, farmers have a strong streak of common sense. They need to be appealed to. Almost all farmers have to borrow during the course of a year, and they should understand the flaws in the Reagan tax program that keep interest rates high. They need to hear that Democrats support the increase in estate exemption, important to family farmers who want to keep a farm together. Their strongest organization, the Farm Bureau, went along with the Reagan program totally, even though prior to this time the Farm Bureau has strongly backed a balanced budget. Democrats have to communicate with farmers. If the party combines that communication with a program that really is designed to help the small family farmer, Democrats can do well, very well.

Hispanics: I am listing Hispanics separately from other nationalities because they are so numerous. Cubans tend to vote Republican, Mexicans and Puerto Ricans Democratic. They have strong family ties, substantial social needs. Unfortunately, the voter turnout in the Mexican and Puerto Rican communities tends to be low. Voter turnout is not likely to become high, but it can improve, and any improvement helps Democrats. More Hispanic people appointed to positions of responsibility by Democrats in state and local government would help.

Jews: A high turnout group, they are strongly Democratic; but a large number voted for Reagan despite what Jimmy Carter had done at Camp David. The Jewish community never fully accepted Carter; some of Billy Carter's remarks hurt. If they see the Democrats with practical programs, Jews should return to the fold in substantial numbers. Both Israel and civil liberties are important to many, for understandable reasons.

Nationalities: Many first- and second-generation Americans still maintain strong ties and interests in the country from which their family came. The interests vary. Lithuanians are concerned that the gallant people of that country, who have endured so much under the Soviets, are not forgotten. Irish are interested in peace and stability in strife-torn Northern Ireland. The list goes on. Sensitivity to problems in other countries is not a strong suit for Americans, but Democrats tend to be better on this than Republicans. We can make some gains.

Outstanding Individuals: This may seem like an unusual category, but as the Democratic party stresses the need for improved quality in our culture, the party should appeal to men and women of talent and force and vitality throughout our society. The nation needs to protect and give opportunity to many, but it also needs to nurture and encourage and challenge an elite, if you will, people of superior potential who sense in the Republican program an appeal to yesterday, an appeal to mediocrity. The importance of bringing this leadership into the Democratic fold can hardly be overstressed.

Poor People: They don't vote in large numbers, but gradually the truth about the present administration is reaching them and should increase the vote. Speaker of the House Thomas "Tip" O'Neill put it well: "The President may be hard as nails when it comes to programs like food stamps and school lunches that help poor people. He may be a real tight wad when it comes to programs like student loans that offer opportunity to our young people. But when it comes to giving tax breaks to the wealthy of this country, the President has a heart of gold."[5]

Professionals: Because of income, most of these groups tend to be Republican, but group by group they should be approached and listened to. Physicians and dentists, for example, who are overwhelmingly Republican, may be hurt by the Medicaid changes. These are people who also have substantial investments and the drop in the stock market of 200 points in the days after it was apparent the Reagan tax program would pass has discouraged some of them. Gains are possible.

Protestants (Conservative Evangelicals): Members of this group tend to be southern and near southern in geography and Democratic by inclination, in part because they tend to be low income, though the income level is rising. Moral Majority and other far-right groups have made headway for the Republicans. The Moral Majority newspaper reportedly has a circulation of one million. The Democrats need to work on the conservative evangelicals and can make an appeal on a religious basis: what Democrats are doing for the elderly, for the handicapped, for families, for neighborhoods, for jobs, and for the poor here and abroad. Because the Moral Majority is lacking in a sensible analysis of basic issues, their welcome mat can wear thin. However, Republicans made big gains in 1980 and hope to do the same in 1982.

Protestants (Mainline): Republican because of economics, they will generally not vote on a religious basis. Civil rights became an issue for some in the sixties, and help for the poor abroad and the arms-control issue have the potential of appealing in 1982 and 1984. The arms-control issue has become big among church people in Europe and is likely to emerge more here. That should help the Democrats. Columnist Gary Wills, a Roman Catholic, comments: "I think that the principal moral issue today is nuclear weapons. That is the area the churches must move into."[6]

Senior Citizens: A high turnout group, they ought to be voting more Democratic in 1982 and 1984. They know the Social Security facts of life and what the Reagan administration has tried to do to them.

Small-Town Residents: They tend to vote Republican. Democrats must begin to communicate with them. "We haven't been reaching small-town America," my colleague, Representative Wes Watkins, says. He is right. Here is a fluid situation, where either the Democrats or Republicans could make gains. Things such as balanced budgets and high interest rates have even more impact than specific small-town programs. And Reagan hostility to revenue sharing should help among thousands of normally Republican officials.

Students: They were a largely nonvoting group in 1980. John Anderson made inroads among those who did vote, but Reagan's student programs, general antieducation stance, plus a student sensitivity in foreign affairs and other areas in which Reagan is not on the same wave length should improve things for Democrats.

Teachers: They are listed separately from professionals and union members because they are increasingly active politically. Many do not agree with their national associations, the National Education Association (NEA) and the American Foundation of Teachers (AFT), on some matters, but the huge majority recognize that the Republican program is not good news for education.

Union members: Republicans made great headway in 1980, but that is not likely to be repeated in 1982 and 1984.

Veterans: The Veterans of Foreign Wars broke tradition in 1980 and endorsed candidates for the first time, generally endorsing Republicans. Many of their members feel they have been stung, for Reagan has let them down. Those who have been in the forefront of the fight for veterans' programs have been such Democrats as Representative David Bonior of Michigan, a Vietnam veteran, and Representative "Sonny" Montgomery of Mississippi. Democrats lost some ground in 1980 that the party should gain back, particularly if there is a jobs program with a veterans preference funded by Democrats.

While serving all of these "tribes," the Democratic party must make clear that it is serving the entire nation, for there is, fortunately, enough patriotism and sense of national purpose that most groups will rebel if they believe they are being catered to and the national purpose is not being served. The young and the old, the poor and the rich, the hale and the infirm should all sense that even as they are being helped, there is also a vision for the nation as a whole.

There are those who will suggest that this book calls for additional spending programs — not what the nation wants. What I call for is a shifting of priorities, a different emphasis. If what is suggested in this book were to be adopted in toto, the expenditure total would not differ appreciably from the Reagan figure, but less would be spent on defense and less each year on interest. And we would become a richer and a more caring country. As programs are examined, the nation's leaders and people might well decide to cut back on some programs and/or to spend a little more for health or jobs programs or other things, and that would not trouble me. Respected conservative columnist George Will has criticized conservatives for being "obsessed by a crude measurement — the percentage of GNP taken by taxes. By that measure, Britain has been much better off than Germany."

Most of the groups I have mentioned should become more Democratic. But Democrats have to learn to "get the message out" without the financial resources of the right wing and the traditional wealthy Republican sources. That makes volunteer efforts even more essential. There are negatives: Reagan's personal popularity and the heavy right-wing mail. Mail specialist Richard Viguerie is probably correct in asserting that even if the Democrats start full scale tomorrow on an effective mail campaign, the Viguerie brand of postal blitz will remain ahead for at least six years. The right-wing mail effort has been like steady drops of water, each seemingly unimportant, but the net effect a political floodwater. Democrats must learn from their example. And if Democrats learn, a Democratic coalition should emerge as a majority in this country.

There is one other reason: government, among other functions, must give people hope. A solid Democratic program that stresses productivity, economic justice, and the improvement of quality in the nation is one to which all Americans can look with hope. The Republican program substitutes nostalgia for hope, a dream of a yesterday that never really was, for a vision of what this nation and this world might become.

Walt Whitman wrote: "It is provided in the essence of things that from every fruition of success, no matter what, shall come forth something to make a greater struggle necessary."[7] Democrats must pursue victory, not for the sake of victory, but for the greater struggle — the chance to make our nation and our world a place of greater hope and freedom and opportunity.

Notes

Introduction
1. Woodrow Wilson, first inaugural address, 4 March 1913.

Chapter One: The Meaning of the 1980 Elections
1. General Social Surveys, conducted by the National Opinion Research Center, University of Chicago, quoted in *Public Opinion,* August-September 1980, p. 28.

2. In Illinois, there were a number of additional presidential candidates on the ballot both in 1976 and in 1980. For these statistics only the Democratic and Republican candidates were compiled.

3. Conversation with Paul Simon, 8 February 1981.

Chapter Two: A Lesson from History
1. Henry Fairlie, "Sweet Nothings," *The New Republic,* 11 June 1977, pp. 17–19.

2. *Federalist Papers,* no. 63, *Great Books of the Western World,* volume 43 (Chicago: Encyclopedia Britannica, 1952), p. 192.

3. Plutarch, *The Lives of the Noble Grecians and Romans,* Dryden translation, *Great Books of the Western World,* volume 14 (Chicago: Encyclopedia Britannica, 1952), pp. 648–49.

4. Quoted in "How Former Presidents Have Used the Polls," *National Journal,* 19 August 1978, p. 1314. No author indicated.

Chapter Three: Needed: A Sense of Concern
1. Statement made in discussion meeting of Democratic members of the House, 31 January 1981.

Chapter Four: Balanced Budgets and Inflation
1. Hobart Rowen of the *Washington Post,* quoted in "Financial Markets Have Little Confidence in Reaganomics," *St. Petersburg* (Florida) *Times,* 6 August 1981, p. 24a.

2. *Second Policy Statement,* by the Committee to Fight Inflation, Arthur Burns, chairman (Washington: American Enterprise Institute, 1980), p. 1.

3. "A Budget of a Thousand Cuts," *Chicago Tribune,* 26 September 1981, p. 10.

4. Buckminster Fuller, *Distinguished Lecture Series,* (Nutley, N.J.: Hoffmann-LaRoche, 1981), pp. 21–22.

5. *World Development Report 1981,* authorized by the World Bank (New York: Oxford University Press, 1981), p. 157.

6. Walter E. Hoadley, "The Emerging International Economic Environment," in *Quest for Peace: American-Japanese Economic Relations,* ed. Susumu W. Nakamura (Hirakata City, Osaka-Fu, Japan: Kansai University, 1979), p. 22.

7. William Niskanen, from speech to the National Association of Business Economists, quoted in a box on the editorial page, *Chicago Tribune,* 26 September 1981, p. 10.

8. "Social Security Choices," editorial, *Washington Post,* 24 August 1981, p. A16.

9. *Summary of Recommendations,* Task Force on Inflation of the House Budget Committee, 6 August 1979, p. 14.

10. Arthur M. Okun, "Inflation: The Problems and Prospects Before Us," in *Inflation: The Problems It Creates and Policies It Requires* (New York: New York University Press, 1970), pp. 31–32.

Chapter Five: Jobs

1. Decree of the French Provisional Government, 25 February 1848.

2. Speech in the Senate, 8 April 1939.

3. Quoted in Milton Meltzer, *Violins and Shovels* (New York: Delacorte Press, 1976), p. 18.

4. Richard Nixon, *Public Papers of the Presidents of the United States* (Washington: U.S. Government Printing Office, 1971), p. 1142.

5. Felix Frankfurter, *From the Diaries of Felix Frankfurter,* ed. Joseph P. Lash (New York: Norton, 1975), p. 175.

6. Milton Katz, "Woodrow Wilson and the Twentieth Century," *Confluence* 5, no. 3 (Autumn 1956):232.

7. Judy Gueron, "The Supported-Work Experiment," in *Employing the Unemployed,* ed. Eli Ginzberg (New York: Basic Books, 1980), p. 86.

8. Ibid., p. 87.

9. *Final Report on the WPA Program, 1935–43* (Washington: U.S. Government Printing Office, 1947), p. iv.

10. There is a variety of ways of roughly calculating the costs. Because of the requirement that beneficiaries should be out of work at least thirty days, approximately half of the eight million unemployed would not be eligible. Of the four million remaining, some would find private employment rather than take the public-service jobs, some would draw benefits under trade-benefit laws or a restructured unemployment-compensation law. Perhaps two million (or at the most three million) would take part. At the peak of the WPA program, three million out of a total of nine million unemployed participated. Assuming two million at a cost per job of $5,500, plus $2,000 per job for supervisory and administrative costs, the total direct outlay would be $15 billion. A rough estimate for budget purposes is that each $1.00 in federal expenditure returns $0.25. That would bring the cost down to $11,250,000,000. There would be some savings on welfare, food stamps, and unemployment compensation that could conservatively be figured at a 10-percent savings, bringing the cost to slightly more than $10 billion. That equals roughly $5 billion per one million public-service employees. If, instead

of two million of the four million eligible, there were three million who would be placed, the cost at most would be $15 billion, because with that high a percentage of participation, other government welfare costs would experience a substantial drop. Two other ways of calculating are to use the CETA costs or the WPA costs of the early 1930s and add the inflation factor. Both of these methods come out at a slightly lower figure, though approximately the same.

When the economy is moving well, the costs will be reduced. The president should be given great flexibility in determining the desirable public-service-employment numbers. A program that would stand rigidly at three million jobs in good times and in bad obviously does not make sense.

11. Richard P. Nathan, "Public Service Employment," in *Employing the Unemployed,* ed. Eli Ginsberg (New York: Basic Books, 1980), p. 71.

12. John H. G. Pierson, *Essays on Full Employment* (Metuchen, N.J.: Scarecrow Press, 1972), p. 69. Taken from a 1944 paper by the author.

13. Peter Hart, remarks to Democratic members of the House of Representatives, Washington, D.C., 31 January 1981.

Chapter Six: Industrial Modernization, Research, and Exports

1. Vernon Louviere, "Let's Rebuild, America!" *Nation's Business* 68 (November 1980):36.

2. Address before the National Press Club, 4 December 1980, mimeo p. 7.

3. Frank Church, speech at Brigham Young University, Provo, Utah, 12 December 1978.

4. Lester C. Thurow, *The Zero-Sum Society* (New York: Basic Books, 1980), p. 87.

5. William Bumgarner, quoted in "How a Japanese Firm is Faring on Its Dealings with Workers in U.S.," by Masayoshi Kanabayashi, *Wall Street Journal,* 2 October 1981, p. 1.

6. Harry Anderson, et al, "The U.S. Economy in Crisis," *Newsweek,* 19 January 1981, p. 30.

7. Paul Recer, "Patent System a Drag on Innovation," *U.S. News and World Report,* 2 February 1981, pp. 45–46.

8. Governor Lee Dreyfus, quoted by Senator William Proxmire in a speech to the Congressional Clearinghouse on the Future, 23 September 1980, *Congressional Roundtable on Emerging Issues,* mimeographed booklet published by the Congressional Clearinghouse on the Future, Washington, D.C., p. 4.

9. Statement made to a meeting of Democratic members of the House of Representatives, 31 January 1981.

10. A. Gary Shilling, quoted in Harry Anderson, et al, "The U.S. Productivity Crisis," *Newsweek,* 8 September 1980, p. 54.

11. Steve Lohr, "The Rise of American Exports," *New York Times,* 25 January 1981, p. 1, section 3.

Chapter Seven: Health Services

1. H. F. Amiel, *Journal,* 3 April 1866.

2. "Mr. Reagan vs. Clean Air," editorial, *Chicago Tribune,* 11 August 1981, p. 10, section 1.

Chapter Eight: Education

1. Aristotle, quoted by Diogenes Laertius, *Lives of the Philosophers,* trans. A. Robert Caponigri (Chicago: Henry Regnery Company, 1969), p. 189.

2. Ronald E. Muller, *Revitalizing America* (New York: Simon & Schuster, 1980).

3. Clark Kerr, quoted in "View From the Bridge," *Time,* 17 November 1958.

4. Testimony before the House Subcommittee on Postsecondary Education, 15 July 1981.

5. William McInnes, "Should Professors Speak in Tongues?" *Change* 13, no. 7 (October 1981):11.

6. Hearings of the Subcommittee on Select Education, House of Representatives, 27 September 1979.

7. James Madison, letter to W. T. Barry, 4 August 1822.

Chapter Nine: Culture and Religion

1. Milton Meltzer, *Violins and Shovels* (New York: Delacorte Press, 1976), p. 142. Congressman is not named.

2. Thomas Jefferson, *The Writings of Thomas Jefferson,* volume I, ed. H.A. Washington (Washington, D.C.: Taylor & Maury, 1953–54), p. 433. Quoted in my remarks before Postsecondary Education Subcommittee hearing in New York City, 2 March 1981.

3. Meltzer, *Violins and Shovels,* p. 79.

4. Ibid., p. 90.

5. Comments during hearings of House Subcommittee on Postsecondary Education, 2 March 1981.

6. Ibid.

7. Testimony before the House Subcommittee on Postsecondary Education, 2 March 1981.

8. Elma Lewis, founder-director of the National Center of Afro-American Artists, New York City; testimony before the House Subcommittee on Postsecondary Education, 2 March 1981.

9. Testimony before the House Subcommittee on Postsecondary Education, 25 February 1981.

10. Wallace Dace, *National Theaters in the Larger German and Austrian Cities* (New York: Richards Rosen Press, 1980).

11. Ibid., pp. 405–6.

12. Ibid., pp. 410–11.

13. Ibid., p. 416.

14. Quoted by Frank Muir, *An Irreverent and Thoroughly Incomplete Social History of Almost Everything* (New York: Stein and Day, 1976), p. 25.

15. Wallace Dace, *National Theaters in the Larger German and Austrian Cities* (New York: Richards Rosen Press, 1980), p. 420.

16. Testimony before House Subcommittee on Postsecondary Education, 2 March 1981.

17. H. de Vere Stacpoole, quoted by Frank Muir, *An Irreverent and Thoroughly Incomplete Social History of Almost Everything* (New York: Stein and Day, 1976), p. 176.

18. Louis Harris, *Americans and the Arts* (New York: American Council for the Arts, 1981), pp. 3–49.

19. Ovid, *Epistulae ex Ponto,* I, volumes 51–80 (New York: G. P. Putnam's Sons, 1924), p. 295.

20. Akinobu Kojima, *Quest for Peace: American-Japanese Economic Relations* (Hirakata City, Osaka-Fu, Japan: Kansai University, 1979), pp. 92–93.

21. Senator Richard Clark, quoted in Charles Austin, "Religious Left and Right Split on Role in Society," *New York Times,* 27 September 1981, p. 30.

22. Quoted in Jere Real, "What Jerry Falwell Really Wants," *Inquiry,* August 3 and 24, 1981, p. 16.

23. Interview with Robert Scheer, "The Prophet of Worldly Methods," *Los Angeles Times,* 4 March 1981.

24. Quoted in Real, "What Jerry Falwell Really Wants," p. 14.

25. Charles Peters, "Religion, Saving Oil and Good News Ahead," *Washington Post,* 24 May 1981, p. C2.

Chapter Ten: Agriculture

1. P. A. Kropotkin, *Paroles d'un revolte,* 1884.

2. Erick Eckholm, *Losing Ground* (New York: Norton, 1976), p. 18.

3. *New York Times,* 12 May 1934, p. 8, column 8.

4. Council for Agricultural Science and Technology, *Conservation of the Land, and the Use of Waste Materials for Man's Benefit* (Washington, D.C.: Government Printing Office, 1975), pp. 16–17.

5. Bob Bergland, *A Time to Choose* (Washington: Department of Agriculture, 1981), pp. 116–17.

6. Ibid., p. 69.

7. Ibid., p. 70.

8. Ibid., p. 122.

Chapter Eleven: The Cities

1. Thomas Jefferson, letter to James Madison, 20 December 1785, *Jefferson Works,* ed. Paul Leicster Ford (New York: G.P. Putnam's Sons, 1894), 4:479–480.

2. Robert Townsend, *Up the Organization* (New York: Knopf, 1970), p. 162.

3. Unsigned report, "In Search of Livable Cities," *Transatlantic Perspectives,* March 1980, p. 13.

4. Eric B. Brettschneider, testimony before House Subcommittee on Select Education, 2 December 1980.

5. Michael Demarest, "He Digs Downtown," *Time,* 24 August 1981, pp. 44–46.

Chapter Twelve: Energy

1. David Stockman, "The Wrong War? The Case Against National Energy Policy," *Public Interest,* no. 53, (Fall 1978), pp. 3–44.

2. Milton Friedman, quoted in *Newsweek,* 4 March 1974, p. 71.

3. Robert Stobaugh and Daniel Yergin, "Energy: An Emergency Telescoped," *Foreign Affairs* 58, no. 3 (1979):592.

4. Ronald E. Muller, *Revitalizing America* (New York: Simon & Schuster, 1980), p. 256.

5. *A National Agenda for the Eighties,* Report of the President's Commission (Washington: U.S. Government Printing Office, 1980), p. 143.

6. Lester Thurow, *The Zero-Sum Society* (New York: Basic Books, 1980), p. 29.

7. I. C. Bupp and Frank Schuller, "Natural Gas: How to Slice a Shrinking Pie," in *Energy Future,* eds. Robert Stobaugh and Daniel Yergin (New York: Random House, 1979), p. 78.

8. R. W. Scott, *World Oil* 186, no. 7 (June 1978), p. 5.

9. Dennis Hayes, quoted by Modesto A. Maidique, "Solar America," in *Energy Future,* eds. Robert Stobaugh and Daniel Yergin (New York: Random House, 1979), p. 183.

10. Jerome B. Wiesner, *Distinguished Lecture Series* (Nutley, N.J.: Hoffmann-LaRoche, 1981), p. 33.

Chapter Thirteen: Defense

1. Robert L. Branyan and Lawrence H. Larsen, *The Eisenhower Administration 1953–1961,* volume II (New York: Random House, Inc., 1971), p. 1350.

2. Pierre Lellouce, "Europe and Her Defense," *Foreign Affairs* 59, no. 4 (spring 1981):830.

3. Lars-Erik Nelson, "Why Are the Russians More Scared of the Bomb Than We?" *Dial,* January 1981.

4. Robert G. Kaiser, "U.S.–Soviet Relations: Goodbye to Detente," *Foreign Affairs* 59, no. 3 (1980):503.

5. *Quoted in* Nikita Khruschchev, *Khrushchev Remembers, The Last Testament,* trans. and ed. Strobe Talbott (Boston: Little, Brown and Co., 1974), p. 412.

6. Vatican Statement to the United Nations, 30 April 1976.

7. September 17, 1979 during debate on Senate floor.

8. Khrushchev, *Khrushchev Remembers, The Last Testament,* pp. 411–12.

Chapter Fourteen: Foreign Policy

1. William H. McKinley, letter to H. G. Otis, 21 December 1898.

2. Press conference, Washington, D.C., 16 June 1981.

3. Interview with the Secretary of State, *Wall Street Journal,* 9 July 1981, p. 24.

4. Chester A. Crocker, quoted in Carl T. Rowan, "Crawling with South Africa," *Washington Post,* 8 September 1981, p. A27.

5. Ibid.

6. Mohammed Riza Pahlavi, *Answer to History* (New York: Stein and Day, 1980), pp. 27–8.

7. Paul Tsongas, *The Road From Here* (New York: Knopf, 1981), p. 167.

8. Carl T. Rowan, "Seeing Beyond the Transiency of a Khadafy," *St. Petersburg* (Florida) *Times,* 29 August 1981, p. 14a.

9. Robert J. Samuelson, "U.S. Exposed to the Whims of the World Marketplace," *National Journal,* 15 September 1979, p. 1517.

10. Unnamed French diplomat, "French Are Right, We're Wrong," editorial, *Chicago Sun-Times,* 2 August 1981, p. 3 of "Views" section.

11. Andrew Young, "The U.S. and Africa," *Foreign Affairs* 59, no. 3 (1980):666.

12. Clark Clifford, *Distinguished Lecture Series* (Nutley, N.J.: Hoffmann-LaRoche, 1981), p. 7.

13. Francis Bacon, "Seditions and Trouble," in *Bacon's Essays with Annotations,* ed. Richard Whately (London: John W. Parker & Son, 1957), p. 137.

14. John Gilligan, statement to the Committee on Agriculture, National Governors' Association, Denver, Colorado, 5 August 1980.

15. Jimmy Carter, *Public Papers of the Presidents of the United States,* Book 1 — January 20 to June 24, 1977 (Washington, D.C.: United States Government Printing Office, 1977), p. 961.

Chapter Fifteen: Presidential Selection

1. George Washington, letter to Benjamin Lincoln, 26 October 1788. From *Writings of George Washington 1745–1799,* volume 30, ed. John C. Fitzpatrick (Washington, D.C.: U.S. Government Printing Office, 1939), p. 119.

2. W. T. Sherman, telegram to John B. Henderson, chairman of the Republican National Convention meeting in Chicago. From *Familiar Quotations,* 14th ed., ed. John Bartlett (Boston: Little Brown & Company, 1968), p. 705.

3. W. T. Sherman, letter to H. W. Halleck, September 1864.

4. Smith Simpson, "For a Parliament in the U.S.," *New York Times,* 31 December 1978, p. E15.

5. William Gillette, "Election of 1872," in ed. Arthur M. Schlesinger, Jr., *History of American Presidential Elections,* volume 2, 1848–1896 (New York: Chelsea House, 1971), p. 1315.

6. Terry Sanford, *A Danger of Democracy: The Presidential Nominating Process* (Boulder, Colorado: Westview, 1981), pp. 140–41.

7. Because of the death of Representative Tennyson Guyer, a special election was held in this strong Republican area. The Democratic convention had voted to withhold funds from any candidate for Congress who does not support the Equal Rights Amendment. The Democratic National Committee was unable to give $5,000 to Dale Locker because he opposed the Equal Rights Amendment, as did his opponent. The Democratic candidate lost by 378 votes. Five thousand dollars probably would have more than made the difference. Although I support ERA and always have, I do not believe in litmus tests on whom the party should support. Following that path there will be many other issues considered significant, and the party will break up on these single-issue matters.

8. Milton S. Eisenhower, *The President Is Calling* (Garden City, N.Y.: Doubleday, 1974), p. 395.

9. Sanford, *A Danger of Democracy,* p. x.

10. Robert S. Strauss, letter to Terry Sanford, 28 April 1980. Quoted in Sanford, *A Danger of Democracy,* p. 133.

Chapter Sixteen: Becoming a Majority Party Again

1. Statement before Democratic members of the House of Representatives, Washington, D.C., 31 January 1981.

2. Thomas B. Reed, "Two Congresses Contrasted," *North American Review* 155, no. 2 (August 1892):227.

3. James David Barber, remarks to Democratic members of the House of Representatives, Washington, D.C., 31 January 1981.

4. Quoted by Gary Orren and E. J. Dionne, "The Next New Deal," *Working Papers* 8, no. 3 (May/June 1981):26.

5. Thomas P. O'Neill, Jr.

6. Garry Wills, "Of Saints and Senators," *Sojourners* 10, no. 2 (February 1981):15.

7. Walt Whitman, "Song of the Open Road," *Leaves of Grass* (New York: Paddington Press, 1976), p. 189.

Index